Andersen to the Throne

Shirley Andersen

Copyright © 2024

All Rights Reserved

ISBN: 9798325074073

Andersen to the Throne

One night after Andy passed away, I had a dream where he was playing his trumpet in heaven with a band. I saw Jesus and God watching over everything from a big desk with TV screens, even though they didn't need them.

There was a speaker system that carried sound all over heaven. At one point, I did or said something funny or silly; Jesus called Andy to the throne. He walked over, and Jesus showed him the screen where I had done something humorous. Andy smiled and exchanged a light conversation with Jesus.

"Look what your wife is doing, Andy."

"Well, you gave her to me, and I love her very much, so it's okay."

After saying this, Andy smiled and went back to playing his trumpet.

This happened a few more times, with Jesus calling Andy to the throne whenever I did something hilarious. I think Andy will be very happy when I join him in heaven, so he doesn't have to keep walking back and forth. This dream also reminded me of something important that I would like to quote:

"My command is this that you love one another, as I have loved you greater love has no man than this, that he laid down his life for his friends.".

-John 15: 12-13

Dedication

I would like to dedicate this book to anyone, male or female, who has at one time or another been sexually, mentally, emotionally, and verbally abused. All of you have my respect, and I acknowledge your pain and suffering, which no one should ever have to endure.

I pray for strength and healing for every person, myself included.

YOU ARE NOT TO BLAME!

Acknowledgment

I would like to thank my family: Cheryl, Joe, Craig, Shelly, Corey, Rachael, sweet little Della, and Caitlyn.

Also, my Church family has loved, encouraged, and prayed for me over the past 4 years, even when they did not know I needed it.

Thank you to Celebrate Recovery. That has helped me heal, and in turn, I pray I can help others as God has helped and directed me.

Thank you, Ella. I think you have put almost as much effort into this project as I have, and I couldn't have finished it without you.

Thank you, Andy, simply for everything, and as you always said and signed, "See you soon."

Jason, I couldn't ask for a better therapist because you have helped me so much. Thank you for all the times you simply said just the right thing to get me back on track with intelligence and love. Thank you so very much.

I needed to write this book as a way to heal but also to help other sexually abused victims or survivors.

About the Author

Shirley was born in California and lived there for 6 weeks. Her parents were ready to move back to Texas after spending 8 years in California, where her Dad was able to find work. She graduated from High School in 1970 and two weeks later married the love of her life, Andy Andersen. Andy was a minister for 38 years in Texas, Massachusetts, and Rhode Island. It was a lively and loving marriage with Andy from Boston, Mass, and Shirley from Texas. Their lives were very different, but much love and respect for each other as they saw them through their differences. Her career was very normal at the beginning, but she advanced quickly to Store Manager for a couple of different retail stores. Within a short time, she quickly became a district manager for Olin Mills Studios.

She is a survivor of childhood sexual abuse as well as emotional, verbal, and mental abuse. She does not want others to go through what she went through, and she could not even speak up as she was threatened and abused. Thus, it's very important to her that no other person has to live with the pain but should raise their voice. She wants to encourage anyone to have the strength and courage to stand up for themselves. They need to stop blaming themselves and seek help. It is never right for the victim to keep hurting because, a lot of the time, "hurt people, hurt people."

She challenges all women and men to speak up and not wait 59 years like she has because "YOU ARE NOT TO BLAME."

Shirley carries on teaching and serving in the Church in Connecticut. She is a survivor of childhood sexual abuse, which is why she wrote this book: to help others by directing them to God.

Another reason she wrote this book was to help people heal. It's very important to her that a person should not live with the pain she has had for so long. She wants anyone who is sexually assaulted to speak up and tell someone. Shirley wants to encourage little girls like her to have the strength and courage to speak for themselves. She wants them to stop blaming their selves and seek help. It is never right for the victim to keep hurting, and she solely focuses on this topic in her book.

She encourages all these women to speak up and explains no one has to wait like she did for 59 years. So, don't stay silent from fear; speak your truth.

This is her life verse:

2 Corinthians 1:4-6 says,

"He always comes alongside us to comfort us in every suffering so that we can come alongside those who are in any painful trial. We can bring them this same comfort that God has poured out upon us, and just as we experience the abundance of Christ's own sufferings, even more of God's comfort will cascade upon us through our union with Christ. If troubles weigh us down that just means that we will receive even more comfort to pass on to you for your deliverance. For the comfort pouring into us, empowers us to bring comfort to you, and with this comfort upholding you, you can endure victoriously the same suffering that we experience."

Preface

It is fascinating to witness how we can be so ungrateful at times and become ignorant of the blessings that we have around us. This book gives an insight into my journey as I have had an eventful life. I had my fair share of ups and downs, yet I did not surrender to my problems and chose never to give up.

It is a story of my optimism and determination as a Christian individual who did not give up when life threw hardships my way. This book is a testimony that even when everything around you seems to be falling apart, your faith in God will help you get through all of it. I have been through a lot in life, be it fighting through health problems or dealing with the loss of someone very dear, but I did not lose hope.

In this book, the readers will not only venture on a rollercoaster of catastrophes I went through in my life but also learn how I fought back with resilience and emerged victoriously because I knew my conviction in the Trinity would guide and protect me. My husband was the biggest support throughout my journey. Even after his passing, God did not leave me alone and gave me a wonderful life full of blessings and gratitude.

Contents

Dedication ii
Acknowledgment iii
About the Author iv
Preface vi
Section 1: My First Life 1
Chapter 1: Birth and Family 2
Chapter 2: Childhood 10
Chapter 3: Death to My Rescue 20
Chapter 4: New Church 32
Chapter 5: Andy 42
Chapter 6: Graduation 53
Chapter 7: Bible College 63
Chapter 8: Salvation and Called to Preach 71
Chapter 9: Surgeries 83
Chapter 10: Rhode Island 96
Chapter 11: Texas 106
Chapter 12: Breast Cancer and COVID 112
Chapter 13: Whitney 122
Chapter 14: Funeral 131
Chapter 15: Texas Again 137
Chapter 16: Moving to Connecticut 142
Chapter 17: My New Calling to My Lord 148

Section 1: My First Life

Chapter 1: Birth and Family

Life, I believe, is what you make of it. Everyone has to play a part in influencing their destiny. I carved my own, but I can tell you this: it wasn't easy. I fell and rose only to fall back hard, but I never let that shake or break my spirit. From a very young age, I saw both of my parents work hard. They never lost hope and always smiled through tough times, teaching me perseverance and tact from the beginning.

I was born on a November morning in California in the year 1951. This differed drastically from my parents as they were both born and raised in rural Texas. My parent's families were very close, and both my mom and dad knew each other most of their lives.

My dad was an admirable young man. He was the second oldest among his siblings; he had three sisters and one younger brother. I never saw or knew my paternal grandfather, as he died before I was born. All I knew was that he was a tall and handsome man, concluding that by looking at a picture my grandmother kept of him. My dad's older sister had eight kids, who I never knew very well since we were not around them much. It is a bit embarrassing to admit this now, but I also had trouble remembering all of their names. We weren't close to any of my father's siblings and rarely met them. Hence, I naturally didn't know about many of my cousins either.

My mom, on the other hand, was the fifth of 9 children. She had four brothers and four sisters. She was a humble woman and lived a fairly simple life. Having lost her mother to cancer early in life, my Mom took up the responsibility of the household as she was the oldest of the girls that were home at that time. Her older sister had married and left home, and so had her oldest brother. So, my mother took care of her younger siblings and ran the house. She woke up every morning earlier than everyone else in the house besides her dad (my maternal grandfather), who had to go to work quite early in the morning. She then cooked breakfast for her dad, cleaned the house, woke her siblings up, ensured the younger ones washed and got dressed on time, and then cooked meals for them. She then walked her brothers and sisters to school. Her youngest sister, who was just at the tender age of 4, would either stay back with my dad's family since they lived close by or be taken by my grandpa to work.

My grandpa worked in construction, building roads and bridges for the county; he was a hardworking man. Upon her return from school, my mom would have a list of chores waiting for her at home. She had the responsibility of her three younger sisters. Grandpa used to tell my mom that if the younger siblings were mischievous or if my mother didn't actively discipline them, then she would get a spanking. She was basically a parent to her younger sisters and brother and would also take care of her two older brothers. To her youngest sister, my mother was the only mother figure she had ever known. In fact, she became a mother figure for all her siblings at the age of thirteen, and she never failed in this role.

During the Second World War, my mom's second oldest brother was drafted and dispatched overseas. When he was allowed to return home, the whole family planned a celebration on his return. Mom's third oldest brother had now been drafted too and had to go overseas very soon. So, this was simultaneously a homecoming and going-away party. Usually, my dad's family was also invited. My paternal grandfather worked at a local gas company. Mom's older brother, who was just drafted, also worked at the same company. My grandfather was on call that day. Just before the party started, he abruptly received a call from the workplace informing him that one of the gas wells wasn't operating properly. He was forced to leave the gathering in order to resolve the issue. As he reached there, he got to work right away. All of a sudden, perhaps due to some technical fault, it exploded, killing him and one other man working with him on-site. It was one gruesome accident that left 2 families and numerous friends mourning.

Dad recalls that my grandfather's body pieces were scattered across the field and had to be recovered from all over the place. Listening to this horrible story as a child and imagining what the scene must have looked like terrified me.

My dad's family and mom's family lived in the same small town, and the news of my grandfather's demise and the whole incident spread like wildfire in the region. My grandfather was a respectable man, loved and adored by everybody. He was a kind, compassionate person who was always there for those in need. So, his death wasn't only heartbreaking for my dad and his family; the whole of the small town was left distraught by his sudden demise. My father inherited many of his personality traits and characteristics, including the love of animals, excellence in athletics, and a strong sense of integrity.

My grandfather loved horse riding. When he passed away, my dad got to keep his horse, which was of dark bay color, with long, black forelocks and little white patches over his eyes. It was a pleasant horse and a quick runner, lovingly raised by my grandfather. My dad shared a strong bond with him, trained him every day after school, and considered him a companion. He even went to school riding it, and the horse would return home by itself. My grandmother would corral it, then would let it out when it was time for it to pick my dad up from school. It was so trained that it would go and wait for my dad outside his school, and my dad would come back home riding it. It was as if they were best friends.

My parents had known each other their whole lives, but it wasn't until they graduated high school that they started dating. They fell in love soon enough, then traveled to the big city where my mom lived with one of her cousins, who was about her age. They worked at Levi Strauss, and my Dad stayed home and commuted to work each day since it was just 22 miles to the bigger city. They married in 1942 by the Justice of Peace back in their small town and then returned to the city. My oldest sibling was born the very next year. Soon after her birth, the family moved to California, where my dad got a really great job as a machinist at a workshop. My oldest brother was born within a year of my sister's birth; in April 1943, I was born some years later.

Just like most families in our town, my parents were also religious. We were brought up in a close-knit household and were disciplined by both of our parents. Nevertheless, my parents were very kind and loving. They attended Church rarely until they moved to California. That's when they started to attend church on Sundays near their California home, and my dad regularly helped the local pastor out, either by taking up church tasks or organizing events or church meetings.

One time, the pastor fell ill, so my dad willingly volunteered to preach at the church. The pastor remained sick for several weeks, and my dad began preaching regularly, continuing his job on the side. Even though the pastor was recovering well, my father wished to continue giving his sermons. He brought his request to the church members, and the church eventually voted on who the pastor should be. It was sad that my dad lost, and they brought the old pastor back soon enough.

This loss broke my dad's heart. He was a passionate man, and preaching was his passion as it brought him solace. He tried his best, but the church downright disallowed him from delivering any sermon. He was so hurt by it that he vowed never to visit that church again. He stood by his vow till his death. I knew he had stopped going to the church, but I never got to know the real reason why he stopped attending until years later when one of my maternal aunts told me about it. Thinking of us as kids and not wanting to cloud our sense of religion, my parents kept this incident to themselves.

Even though I was born in California, I had only spent six weeks of my infancy there as my parents were ready to move back to Texas. I recall Andy making a joke about it years later when we were at a Boston Red Sox game, sitting in the bleachers. Andy was reading the program when he said, "You'll never believe this. Dwight Evans, the Boston right fielder, was born on the same day, month, and year as you". My husband teased that Dwight & I could have spent the night together. However, he was born in Santa Monica, and I was in Pasadena. Also, it would have been the hospital nursery as babies, not anywhere as adults.

Dad had secured a job as a night foreman at a machine workshop back in Texas. His job gave him a little time to work with tools and their design and one day. He designed a new tool that would make work easier for oil rig workers. He was responsible for both modifying and repairing them. We lived in Fort Worth, Texas, for the first six years of my life until the shop he was working in closed, and Halliburton transferred those who wanted to move.

Dad then transferred with a few other men to Duncan, Oklahoma. He was an intelligent man and self-aware, too. He was smart enough to teach himself a lot of things, for instance, how the mathematical computer called slide rule works and complex concepts of mechanical system design. The company Dad worked in promoted him to its research and development department as he had already designed and patented one mechanical tool and was working on another.

He had an interest in rodeo as far as I could remember. He would get involved in this dangerous sport even after he married my mom. He just loved the thrill of riding bulls and bare-back broncs. He had taught himself how to best ride those animals and knew the exact time to sit and spin with these animals. He would skillfully move with them, being able to predict the animals' next move and where they were headed, so he knew how to control them. He used to say that he never fought against them, just with them. After a few years of being marginally involved in the competitions, Dad decided to start rodeo clowning. By 1960, he had been working with big-name rodeo clowns like Freckles

Brown in Oklahoma. At the same time, working in his research department allowed him to develop and patent three more mechanical tools in his name.

I would spend 2 to 4 weeks of my summer holidays with my maternal grandfather and his second wife and the rest of the summer with my paternal grandmother. Grandpa was re-married to a younger woman. Even though she was a few years younger than her husband, she loved him to bits and was a sweetheart, making us all adore her. I would frequently go to church with her, and we would always have fun. But it was not as fun as in the church I went to with my paternal grandmother.

My paternal grandmother, or as we all used to call her endearingly, "Mama Tops," was my favorite person in the world. Mama Tops was experiencing some health challenges as she was diagnosed with Parkinson's disease. It is a brain disorder that makes the body tremble. Hence, Mama Tops had trouble balancing herself because of the sickness and occasionally fell. As time went by, Mama Top's condition worsened, and she found it more and more difficult to live alone; she needed someone to look after her constantly, which is why I spent my entire summers with Mama Tops at her house in the small rural town. Then, my Dad's sister, who was next to the youngest, moved in with her daughter and lived with her for the rest of her life.

All in all, I can say that my upbringing was influenced by how my parents were brought up as children. My dad was an inspiration. He was kind and caring but also intelligent and tough. Watching his relentless work ethic and achieving so much made me believe in the fruits of hard work. My mom was a strong and determined woman who took it upon herself to run the house and look after her younger siblings after she lost her mother. She set an example of being selfless. She was a nurturer, and I am lucky to have inherited her positive traits.

Chapter 2: Childhood

"For I know the plans I have for you, declares the Lord, plans for welfare and not for evil, to give you a future and a hope."

-Jeremiah 29:11

Childhood is associated with home, a place where you grow up and spend most of your life and learn how to walk and talk and grow into a beautiful human being. But what exactly is home? A four-wall structure constructed with bricks and cement? Maybe several coats of matte finish paint will make it look appealing—bedrooms, dining room, lounge, kitchen, a small fireplace, and a garden. Then, to make it look fancier, add amenities, such as a little chandelier over the ceiling, sparkly lamps, attractive showpieces, a mini couch, kitchenware, and so on. But is it actually what a home is? Do these pillared walls and the things within them define it? No! Home is not about these material things; instead, it is about the people living in it who make a house a HOME.

It is humans that add value to the place and make it worth loving. A loving mother, hard-working father, extra-caring grandparents, and cute little kids wandering around here and there, creating troubles for the elder ones, describe a home - a picture-perfect family. And that is the true essence of home – the feeling of coziness and warmth. A place where you are welcomed and appreciated. A place that doesn't feel like a prison or where you are not chained and always accepted. And most importantly, home is the place that molds your childhood.

> *"A house is made of walls and beam; a home is filled with love and dreams."*
>
> *-Ralph Waldo Emerson*

Childhood is the most innocent phase of one's life. It is the time when these little ones evolve, learn to differentiate between good and bad, and grow into their own person. It is the foundation upon which the future of a kid depends. It molds their personalities, thought processes, and behavior, all alike; it is also the phase where they sketch out their individualities and talents.

Childhood is supposed to be free, fun, and one of the best times of our lives because that is when we make most of our memories. Those memories bring smiles to our faces when we reminisce about them in later years.

Thousands of miles away from stress and worries, childhood is all about peace, being unbothered and free from worldly issues. It is the time that makes our adulthood special as we allow innocence and helpful nature to take over, giving everyone a message of peace, love, and humanity.

Childhood is undoubtedly the golden stage of anyone's life, laying the groundwork for your future self. But what should it be like? It should be a time of wonder, protection, and care. It should help define oneself and find their goals, dreams, passions, and talents. It should be the centric pillar that focuses on a child's well-being. But sadly, it is not like that for every kid out there. For certain, it is like walking in Disneyland, but then again, not one person is like the other. There are some people for whom it is a journey full of thorns. The scripture in Jeremiah was what God intended for me. However, that part of my life started several years later. He needed to make me the strong person that I needed to be, so I had some difficult years to go through, with God not allowing anything He wouldn't give me strength for.

For me, all these would have, could have, and should have never worked, and my childhood was nothing less than a nightmare. It was something that one wouldn't wish upon even their enemies: a combination of sad and gloomy events, and I hated it. The worst part was that I never got to live any of it, as a cloud of fear and fright followed me wherever I went.

It saddens me as childhood is when we are young and crave the most attention and love from our parents. It is the phase where we want to be seen and noticed. But nothing of the sort happened to me. My entire childhood, I longed for the love and affection of my parents. I wanted them to hear me out and care for me as other parents do for their kids, but I was practically nonexistent to them. They always sent me off to my grandparents rather than giving me the attention I needed and wanted.

When I say I had a terrible home life, it is because of the mental torture and physical abuse I had to endure daily. And it didn't stop there; things took a wild turn later, and I had to go through much more. It all reached a magnitude that will give you chills and leave you speechless. You will know once I talk about the further atrocities of my life.

I wouldn't call us very rich, but my dad made good money. We owned about 50 acres of land, and there was a little creek running alongside. I would find my way toward the creek and lean on the wide branches whenever I was distressed. Indeed, nature has always been the best healer.

My siblings never really liked me, and we were always fighting. Their mind would constantly work to plot against me. And all of that vendetta and fake complaints got me a heavy share of spanking. Whatever they said was believed right away, and my Mom thought they were always right. And then she would get mad and unleash her anger on me.

The worst thing about my childhood was how my family treated me. My mom and sister always made fun of me and were the first to pass nasty comments. You wouldn't expect that from a mother, but believe it or not, she was the first one to abandon me when I needed support.

***

All the other kids around got to live their childhood; they were sent to school, they made friends, and they were allowed to go outside to play, but I didn't have any such liberties. I wasn't like those other kids. My day was regulated around verbal torture and emotional abuse, and this harsh reality grounded me, leaving me helpless.

My sister and I stayed away from each other as much as possible. She didn't like me, and I wasn't fond of her either. She basically envied me and would always say things like, *"We had the perfect family until you were born."* My eyes would fill with tears, and I would run toward the creek, trying to find shelter in the woods.

***

The only exciting thing in my life was my summer vacation. That's when I got to see the people who loved me selflessly. The connection between a grandchild and his grandparents is so beautiful it can never be described in words. It goes beyond explanation, and that's how my relationship was with my grandparents. They both adored me, and I was more connected to them than my parents.

During the summer, I spent at least two weeks with my grandpa (mother's dad) and the rest of the time with my Mama Tops. That time with my grandpa would be so much fun. He lived with his second wife, who was a little younger than him. However, she loved and took great care of my grandpa and me whenever I stayed with them. I often went to church with them, and my grandpa taught me how to pray.

Grandpa lived in a cozy cottage, and they had a huge garden that I loved the most, as I treated it as my playground; I remember learning so many physical games there. Other than playing, I would also help my grandfather with farming and would pick out the ripe vegetables from there. He would also take me to the neighborhood to deliver these vegetables. It would always thrill me as a kid, and I felt involved.

We would play card games and dominoes at night, and if a baseball game were on, we would listen to the radio or watch it on TV. We would hoot whenever our favorite team would score and make booing noises when the opposite team got a point. It was always exciting to enjoy baseball with him. We even used to play baseball in the garden; those were fun times.

My maternal grandfather's unwavering affection for me made me joyful whenever I stayed with him, and I valued his love greatly.

It would always be fun being around Grandpa, but I wouldn't say I liked it as much as spending time with Mama Tops (Dad's mother). She was the best grandmother anyone could ask for. Tops was her last name before marrying my grandfather, so she became Mama Tops since then.

I thought of myself as the fortunate one since I was the only child permitted to stay at both of my grandparents' homes, but oh, how I wish I had known the reality then. I realized years later it had to have been God's protection of me to get me away from my family and be safe even for a few months.

Mama Tops was my favorite person in the whole world, and I will always be grateful to her for everything she taught me. I assisted Mama Tops with various household chores whenever I visited her, including doing laundry with her on a classical washing machine. It was way too ancient and had a handle at the top that you had to spin in order to drain the water while the clothes pressed through. I would hang them outside in the yard to drain the water and then leave them to dry. Mama Tops would typically pull out a chair in the kitchen, and I'd stand on it at the counter to retrieve items, ingredients, and other things while I assisted her in cooking. She also taught me how to prepare delicious meals, including recipes I still use.

Mama Tops was facing some troubles since she had been diagnosed with Parkinson's disease, which caused her hands to tremble. She could hardly walk, so my dad got her a wheelchair.

She always had grey hair and was overweight, weighing around 260 lbs.

Mama Tops would read the Bible to me before sleeping; it was a kind of ritual we would follow whenever I went to her place during the summers. This practice was always helpful for me. She assured me that if I prayed to Him and asked for His help, God would be willing to hear me, as He loves me and would look after me. Her teachings about God and religion made me feel content and at peace. I wondered how such instructions could bring peace to an individual to such an extent, and I could only figure it out as I followed God's path. I complied with the commandments of God.

I prayed for feelings of love to be created within the hearts of my parents and siblings as I felt abandoned and unwanted.

When I got a little older and started watching TV, I quickly realized that my family was nothing like the happy families I saw in sitcoms. Though they appeared satisfied, collected, and amiable, things were actually awful. And I, being the youngest of the clan, was left feeling uneasy and sad every hour of the day.

I was 10 when I realized that things in my family had started to fall apart, and I was always an outsider. I felt like I didn't belong, and the family had no space for me. The irony was that my mother made me go through this turmoil more than anything. It always felt like she liked my sister more than me, and the things she would say weren't easy to hear.

Once, she questioned me, *"Why can't you be intelligent like your sister or good-looking like your brother?"*

I responded, *"I think I will be funny like my dad,"* and then grinned, even though her words hurt me more than they ever had. As a young child, hearing all of this would cause a stinging sensation.

However, my father was a nice guy. He always took care of me and protected me in various circumstances. When I started being good at sports, my father loved it and often helped me play. He was literally like a knight in shining armor, and his jolly nature always brought smiles to everyone's face. He was the comedian of the family and loved cracking dad jokes and doing pranks that would make everyone burst out laughing.

At one family reunion, my dad placed a plastic vomit on the pecan pie that my aunt (my mother's youngest sister) had made. She yelled as she yanked out the pie and stared at it. She looked at my father and chased him outside, inside, and out in the yard because no one could eat it, and my aunt ran after him while laughing uncontrollably. She spent around 15 to 20 minutes chasing him, holding a butter knife. The house echoed in a wave of laughter. And that's how my dad was - always the funniest person in the room.

My sister was highly intelligent. Other than receiving numerous scholarships and outstanding marks, she was never grateful for anything. She never respected me or made me feel like I was her sister, only calling out for me when she needed something. Her behavior toward me always left me confused; some days, she was sweet to me, and on other days, not so much; it all depended upon her mood. If she were happy, then she would be pouring her sweetness, which was also venomous to an extent, but that version was much tolerable. However, if she felt sad or angry, she would lash out at me and treat me like a trash can. I hated that I couldn't say anything or complain because I thought if I complained about her, it would make my parents angry, and they would get rid of me. This idea scared me the most.

My sister would often say that they were the ideal family until I was born, and then a vile, evil smirk would follow. She would get rude and often say that I broke their perfect family when I was a young child, making me feel guilty and sorry. That's where all the self-doubt and insecurities spawned from.

Sometimes, I'd ask Mama Tops why my mother and my father would leave me with her for the entire summer, and her response was one that no child could ever imagine.

She told me they intended to take a little break from me, which is why they would leave me with either my maternal grandfather or Mama Tops. It would sink my heart in sorrow, feeling the pain and hurt rushing through my body.

Often, I sobbed bitterly in my room and pondered why my parents would treat me this way, feeling that my own family had betrayed me, and it hurt like hell. Never in a million years had I thought that my family would ever do this to me. I had no one to confide in, and my family was not even mine.

Whenever I'd think about it, it would shatter my heart into a million pieces. My mind would replay my conversation with Mama Tops, and I would try to divert it somewhere else, but nothing ever helped. All those words would play in a constant loop in my head, and there was no escape. My mind was always cluttered with questions, and all of them led to only one answer: "I am a disappointment!"

Life is an untold truth of agony and ambiguity. If you are lucky enough to experience its positivity, express gratitude. But when something is unfair, there is nothing you can do but accept it for what it is and move on, which is what I did. It was hard, but I tried to make peace with it because I knew there was no way out. I mean, what could I have done instead of crying? So, I just accepted the things as they were and reprimanded myself for mistakes I had never made.

Chapter 3: Death to My Rescue

Life – one word with so many definitions. Every person has their own way of explaining life, and it is often quite different, varying from person to person. Some feel a jolt of rush as they think about it and recall the past moments. For them, it is like a shiny crystal ball, full of fun and joy. Every day is such a blast for them that they can hear the happiness within their own heartbeats. But it doesn't mean it is the same for everyone, as certain people have different takes on life. They feel it is like an ocean, which can either sail you through the other corner or drown you. So, they are considerate and take every step in this journey very wisely. Then, finally, there comes a certain fragment of individuals who think life is just a mess and every aspect of it is emotionally abusive. I was one of those, feeling like that and thinking like that because my life was nothing less than a dark web of lies, suffering, pain, hurt, and shallowness.

When we moved to Oklahoma, it was not that bad. I was excited to see what the new place would bring into our lives. At the same time, I was also hoping this new house would get me the attention and love that I craved so deeply.

One of the things I loved at first when we moved to Oklahoma was the farm and the animals. The farm was quite big – full of greenery. It had all those big trees and plants. Some of those trees also had fruits in them, and I used to pluck them once in a while. It also had such beautiful flowers that I had never seen before. A few of them looked so magical and exotic, especially that blue-tinted one with a splash of red from the inside. It smelled like candy floss, and I would pick one every time I went to the farm. Then, there were the animals - lots of animals, including horses, hens, rabbits, and pigs. I particularly loved one of the pigs that followed me around everywhere. I would run around and play with that little animal. That pig was the first friend I made on the farm, and we both enjoyed each other's company a lot.

To escape the cruelties of my world, I found a shelter on the farm where I spent most of the evenings while we were in Oklahoma. I would run to chase the chickens, cling to the trees, aim stones at the fruits, and play with the animals - especially that goat. It was like a daydream, far from all the pain and hurt. Little did I know that it would soon turn into my worst nightmare.

Initially, the farm was my brother's responsibility – to look after it, especially the animals, but then he got an old car that he started working on with Dad, so it was quite time-consuming. And then, in a few weeks, he also got a job. He was just fourteen when he started working at a grocery store located on the block nearby. He was quite enthralled about it and wouldn't stop bragging about his work and the mates there. All of us were happy for him, and it was good to see him take responsibility on his own. But that wasn't even one percent of the actual reality. He was happy, but the work and his mates weren't the only reason. It was only years later that we found out that the store owner would hitch him with some beers once in a while and would call it his payment for the day.

He was quite young around that time, around 14, and that old grocery owner lured him into his trap, and that's how he stepped into this dark trail. And then it kept pulling him more and more toward it like a spiral. From drinking once in a while to making it a habit, he became an alcoholic. He allowed it to feed on his emotions, which grew that void within him more and more. The worst part was that we weren't aware of it until later on, and then we couldn't do anything because the damage was already done.

I began to witness a slight behavioral change in my brother toward me. He started being skeptical and acting weirdly around us. Initially, whenever I would go to the farm, I would just hover around there and play. But then, since he started working, the responsibility to feed the animals landed on me.

I didn't mind it at all because I loved spending time at the farm and adored all the animals. Initially, it was pretty fun until things got ugly. I fed the animals the first few days with my brother's help and guidance, but I sensed a weird tension between us. He would give those inappropriate looks, and it would always leave me puzzled. It made me uncomfortable, so I decided that I wouldn't wait for him and would feed the animals myself after getting back from school. But he didn't like that and got all riled up, saying that I only needed to do that with him, under his watch. That was the day when he did the vilest thing a brother could ever do to a sister. And to make it worse, I was practically a child – an underaged one.

It was a Wednesday noon; I had just come back from school and was waiting for my brother to return from his baseball game practice so we could go and feed the horses. That was the first time he made a move on me, and I couldn't comprehend it in words. I couldn't even write down my feelings because I was crumbled up.

As we were feeding the horses, he did things that weren't appropriate at all. He asked me to touch his private parts, and I was taken aback because it was a heinous act. I refused as it made me feel awful, but he forced me into doing it anyway. Then he groped me and rubbed himself on me. It was so pathetic to even think about it, let alone to do it. And what is even more disgusting is that I was his little sister. He was seven years older than me, so if he was 14, I was 7.

I didn't know what I was supposed to do. I was blank and tried stopping him, knowing it was wrong, but I was shattered to the point of not knowing how to respond. However, I still threatened him and said I would tell our father about it.

He held my wrist tightly and locked my face in his right hand, squeezing my jaw. Looking right into my eyes, he said, "If you ever say a word to Dad, I will shoot his skull open."

It was hard to think it was a bluff because my brother was deranged and twisted. Post alcoholism, he had turned into this vicious monster – one I was unable to recognize.

After intimidating me, he gave me a broad grin, winked at me, and left the farm singing something.

Those words traumatized me and haunt me to this day. I was already going through a turmoil of emotions, and now there was something even more extreme. That experience was bone-chilling, and no one could ever understand the things I went through and the emotions I felt at that point. I was harassed, and there was no one I could go to, no one I could confide in. I was alone. However, on many days, I would feel a hand holding mine. I've felt that hand many times and almost always when I was going through something traumatic. I've never been able to think it was anyone else, but God showed me he was there for me and never let things get too bad. This whole incident left me shaken up, and I couldn't stop shivering. Tears kept flowing from my eyes like water coming from a loosened tap. I was shattered and felt disgusted. It was the first time I felt so much hatred for my brother in my life. My mother and sister kept creating trouble for me, but this was on another level.

***

I was very young when it all started happening to me. I was seven and had no way of knowing what to do at that time. My brother would casually talk to me about sex and used different movie situations to make me think it was normal to do all that he was doing to me. All those movies objectified women and showcased how they dolled up for men and wore those shiny gowns, for them to be torn apart later. I didn't enjoy the references, and it would twist my insides, but my brother never knew when to stop.

One night, he showed me a movie in which a woman was dressed up in a pretty sexy look and was wearing pearls while cooking, cleaning, and serving her husband. Whatever he said, her moral duty was to do it without any discussion. Eventually, a scene came up where it was pretty dark in the night, and the husband asked the kids to go to bed, took his wife's hand, and led her upstairs. Suddenly, an advertisement interrupted the movie, but my brother was so engrossed in it that he didn't even notice me as I ran out of the room.

The next day, down at the creek, we tied a rope to the tree and were swinging back and forth on it.

As I played, he asked me, "What do you think happened last night when the husband took his wife to bed early?"

I didn't respond.

He waited for a while and then moved his lips temptingly. "They were kissing and taking each other's clothes off. Then, within no time, they were wrapped into one another."

He touched his crotch and said with a wide smirk on his face. "Come here, and I'll show you."

I told him no, in a heavy tone, and turned in another direction.

He walked toward me and threatened me. "Yes, you will, or I'll show you the worst. You will never say no to me again, then."

He then proceeded to lock my wrist in his hand with a strong grip and explained what he would like to do to me and how he would do it. He was pretty precise with what he liked and wanted it the exact way, or else I would get punished. I was always scared and petrified of him because I knew he was a crazy psychopath and could go to any extreme to get what he wanted, so I always gave in. However, it used to kill me from the inside. It wasn't easy to see my brother doing all those horrible things for his own pleasure. I was always this pleasure-seeking machine for him. And he was nothing less than an animal. Actually, even animals were way better than him.

***

A week after that incident, we went to the rifle range with Dad. I was the first one to shoot, and when Dad went to check the target, he was quite impressed. Then it was my brother's turn, and he was his imbecile self as always, but he didn't want to let go of this opportunity either. Instead of shooting at the target, he aimed for a bird in the sky, which we weren't allowed to do, but he did it anyway. My father was enraged and got extremely mad and took us back home.

After we got home, it was almost time to feed the animals, so my brother told me to go right away.

"You should go; I will join a bit later," I knew what was coming, so I whispered in a low voice.

"I ain't requesting or asking for advice. I am ordering, so stand up, or I will smack you!" He shouted.

There was a thunder in his voice, and it worked its way through me. I was petrified and wore a cloak of terror as I followed him through the farm.

While we were feeding, he turned toward me and spoke his disgusting mind, "You think that was an accident; you're wrong. I was warning you. If you ever tell anyone about anything, the outcome won't be good."

There was a slight pause, and then he continued again, "And don't even think of telling Dad. I have warned you before; consider it the last one, or I will kill Dad."

I knew he could do anything, and I didn't want my dad to die. He was the only person who loved me and made me feel welcome. I couldn't let anything happen to him. So, I shook my head in agreement while my entire body was covered in chills. Then he rubbed his hands on my back and left the field. I was left standing there alone, with tears swimming in my eyes. I just wanted the land to burst wide open and swallow me whole.

***

Once my brother got his license, he bought an old Ford Station wagon and worked on it to finally get it running. There were many times when he took me with him, saying that he would drop me off at school but then would drive farther across the country road and ask me to give him pleasure. He would park the car somewhere around a bush or the corner and make me perform sexual acts on him. This didn't happen just once or twice; there were several instances when he did this to me. He would even lie to Dad and would brilliantly cover his tracks. He was a sick and twisted mastermind.

It eventually started happening frequently. My brother would even ask me to touch and rub him while driving the car. I had no other choice but to follow his lead. Due to this, I would often be late for school, which my principal started noticing. He called my mother and asked her why I was coming in late.

My mother didn't know the answer to that question, so she stalled the principal by saying it wouldn't happen again.

However, she didn't question my brother at all. He was the one picking me up and dropping me off. She didn't even think that if we were leaving for school on time, what was causing the delay? It was the right moment to counterattack and ask questions. Instead, my mother just told him to drop me off at school on time. And those words were even wrapped in sugar and honey; that's how sweet her tone was. There was no question, nothing, just this little advice.

This gave him more power and courage to do it. My brother wasn't scared at all now and felt entitled to carry out the atrocious acts every chance he got. And when I would cry like a helpless baby in front of him, he would put it all on me. He would tell me that it was all my fault. He often even said that it was his privilege as a man to treat me or any female as he pleased. There was no way I could ever say anything. So, it kept going on like that for a while.

***

After years of crushing my soul and body, his torture finally stopped one day around October 1963. I should have been happy to get rid of him, to put a stop to my misery, but instead, that phase of my life made me sad and numb because in the same month, my father died, and I lost the only person who cared for me and protected me.

My life had become a mess. Every day, there would be a new problem waiting for me. Every time I tried to move on from the wounds of the past, another bullet would rip my skin open.

My Dad had a heart condition, and the doctor said he had an irregular heartbeat and a high heart rate. That's why he couldn't even make it to the Navy. He knew about his heart condition all his life and didn't tell any of us or get it treated. He thought it was just a minimal issue and would improve in time, so he kept neglecting it.

Then, in the summer of 1963, he started playing softball for his company. Since he was a tall man, he usually hit a home run or strikeout in the game. This meant he always had to be on the defensive spot and didn't have to run except for that one game.

And it turned out to be the death ringer. It was quite a charged-up game, and my Dad gave it his all. But then, after the game was over, he came home panting. He was completely out of breath and faced difficulty inhaling or exhaling the air.

I had seen him like that for the first time – helpless and tired. He came and sat by Mom and leaned back until he could breathe better. After a while, he started feeling better, so he still didn't go to the doctor. All of us kept forcing him to go and get checked as he had just been out of a terrible condition. But he was persistent and kept saying that he was fit and okay.

Everything stayed fine for a while, but then, in October, his heart condition relapsed. That night, he couldn't sleep, feeling like he had a heartburn. But when his condition got worse, my brother drove Mom and Dad to the hospital at about 1:30 am. I was so worried that I kept pacing around my room out of stress, praying for my father's health and recovery.

Around 4:00, my mom and my brother returned home, and Mom just said, "Your Father is dead." There wasn't even a single scrunch or hesitation on her face. She just walked in and said it like she was announcing something unimportant.

'How do you say something like that so calmly?' I thought to myself as tears began to fall down my face. I was upset with how she had told this news to my sister and me. I kept waiting for her to console us or hug us, but there was no extra emotion from her side.

Thankfully, Mom's best friend Joyce, her husband, and her youngest son were right behind them, and they walked through the door just as she had revealed this news to us. Joyce was very close to me and adored me with all her heart. She came to me, hugged me, and then took me to my bedroom. She caressed my head, held me, and let me cry in her arms, something Mom would never do. It was a hard night for me, and I cried myself to sleep, but the next day turned out to be a lot harder as we would bury my father. It was something that left me completely broken.

The funeral was held the next day, and the house was cluttered with guests. It was hard for me to stay in the house and sit there. Joyce asked Mom if she could take me away from all this for a little while. Mom agreed, and Joyce and her son Ron took me out.

Then, as we reached their house, Joyce said she was tired, but Ronny & I could go out if we wanted. Ron and I were the closest friends, and he understood me like no one else. So, he thought it was a great idea to clear my head, and so he took me to the park. We went to the nearby park in town and just talked our hearts out. Then, as I cried, he held me, and I poured it all out to him while he listened to my ugly cries. I can never forget how he was there for me in the worst phase of my life, and I could never thank him enough.

Then we drove back to the house, took Joyce, and went back to my house. Going back, I was sad and devastated because Dad was the only one who cared for me. And now, with him gone, I didn't know what would happen to me. My brother was there, too, so it was stressing me out. It was all a bit too much for me, but Joyce said she was just a call away, and Ron said he was there too, so it gave me strength.

After my dad's funeral, things drastically changed for me. I thought my brother would get more brutal with his heinous acts, but he didn't. It all changed 180 degrees as he decided to join the Army. Initially, we all thought he was just playing around, but after his training,-he went to Vietnam. The physical and sexual abuse that I was subjected to by him stopped. Over time, I forgave him because I thought it was the alcohol that had turned him into this vile creature. So, I let go of all the baggage from the past and tried to move on.

Eventually, my sister went away from home as well, and started college, and then got married. So, then, it was just my mom and I who were left behind, leading to a fruitful outcome. Our relationship organically bloomed during that time, and we both grew closer to one another. After a while, we decided to move to her old hometown. Both my mother and father talked a lot about that place and shared all those amazing memories they had kept close to their hearts. For the first time in my life, I was excited to see what the future holds.

"Wherefore comfort yourselves together, and edify one another, even as also ye do."

-Thessalonians 5:11

Chapter 4: New Church

"This is the day the Lord has made, let us rejoice and be glad in it."

-Colossians 3:12

The place where you are born and raised holds the most special place in your heart. That old house where you learn how to walk, the pavements where you fall so many times while learning how to peddle around and park right across the main street that witnesses your giggles. Nothing can beat the warmth of your hometown and its memories. For my mother, her hometown was also like a splatter of sunshine. She had lived her best life there, and now, I was pretty enthralled to be visiting that fragment of her life that always made her feel on top of the world.

With all our affairs in Oklahoma sorted, my brother was off to Vietnam to serve in the military, and my sister was moving out for college with her future husband; it was just me and my mother left behind. We were planning to move out quite soon as well. We started packing and gave away the things that we didn't want to take with us. It took us a couple of days to pack and organize all our stuff.

After we were all packed and ready to leave, my mother rented a U-Haul truck for a day to help with the shifting. Since there were a lot of things, and we couldn't load it all by ourselves, we needed some help. Luckily, Joyce and Ron were there to lend us their support.

After loading everything, we were finally ready to kick-start our journey. Ron drove the truck, and I went with him while my mom and Joyce were in their cars. Joyce took the car so she and Ron wouldn't have to struggle on their way back.

As we were getting closer to the destination, my heartbeat intensified. I was excited and nervous at the same time. I didn't know what this new place would be like and what opportunities it would bring for me. However, I had a feeling that this move was going to prove really lucky for us both.

It was a bigger city just about 20 miles away from where Mom and Dad grew up. The city was densely populated and housed around 125,000 residents. The infrastructure of the place was quite admirable, and all the residential units were finely constructed. Around the edge of the town, there was an Air Force base.

Fate rolled the dice in our favor as we had found a nice house by the lake. It was small and cozy on the opposite side of town from the base, and it came furnished with some vintage furniture. The best part was that this new place was quite secluded, far from chaos. That's why settling there wasn't that difficult, and we adjusted swiftly to this new atmosphere.

It was a good, fresh start, and things transitioned pretty smoothly. My relationship with my mother was healing, and now she had started treating me better. I think her positive real side was shining out brightly, and there was no one to dampen it, as the negative influence of my sister was gone from her life. I was very happy with this new change.

Our days were spent catering to routine activities. My mom instantly got a job, and she started working part-time in a fabric store while I was enrolled in high school as a freshman. It was a different experience as this school wasn't like the previous ones. People were more accepting, the staff was quite cooperative, and the academic curriculum was balanced, too. All these factors made fitting in this new environment pretty easy.

As the year progressed, I introduced myself to different sports and explored my athletic side. There was a different game for every season. During the warmer months, they used to run track. In winter, it was basketball, and during the summers, everyone was really into softball.

Among these sports, softball was my favorite, and I was surprisingly okay with it. I played catcher and, to some degree, controlled the entire game, calling what pitch the pitcher would throw next. We had a good team, and all of us played really well together- winning most of the games.

When I was a junior, they had a really good pitcher on the team, who was good. She was a senior and bagged good reviews in every game she played. She was like a strong force.

It was the last game of the year when the scout from Oklahoma State University visited our school and watched the game. It was a playoff, and winning the game would take us to the finals. That day, after the game was over, the scout didn't sign her as the pitcher but promised me a letter for a full ride to OSU as a catcher.

***

There was a small church close to where we lived. Mom and I started going there every Sunday morning. It was a peaceful experience. It was a feeling I can't express in words. My mother also felt that it was like a spiritual detox. Since we both find the church quite comforting, we started visiting more often – twice or three times a week. Going there often also brought a really positive change in her. It made her understand her responsibilities. For the first time, she had started acting like an actual mother.

Frequently visiting church impacted me as well and allowed me to get closer to God. It also helped me channel the inner abilities that were hidden deep down somewhere. It was encouraging me to become a better version of myself. It blessed me with a positive newness. I was able to get out of the darkness and become hopeful again. It all happened because of the church, so I started investing more time there. Later, I got to be a part of teen meetings at church and sang in the choir every Sunday morning.

One of those Sundays, I was singing in the choir when a really cute Air Man from the base walked in. It was at this moment I thought I heard the Holy Spirit say, "He's the One!"

It was Andy. The morning he and I met, when he walked into church with his roommate, who was the son of a preacher outside of St. Louis, Missouri, I couldn't help but notice how handsome he was. He looked quite attractive in his uniform; his appealing smile, deep blue eyes, and silky blonde hair bounced in the air as he walked slowly, all adding to his charm.

The church always had us all meet the guys from the base to welcome them, and that's how I met Andy for the first time. The first glance was enough to help me realize he was special. He was the most handsome man I have ever met, and he was very soft-spoken. I felt an immediate connection with him. It was as if I knew him; we had been connected for ages. We would start talking and go on to talk for hours, and still, it wasn't enough.

After church was over, we were introduced to each other. He had such a strong Bostonian accent, and his voice was making it more appealing. It was hard to focus on anything else other than his face, but I tried my best to stay focused. He told me about his background; he was born and raised in Boston, Massachusetts. I was like, 'That's very far from her'. Then, I told him I had never been to anywhere except Texas and Oklahoma.

As we talked after-church that day, a weird thought popped into my head and took a huge proportion of my mind. Little did I know, our feelings were mutual.

After that day, it was in no time that we found out everything about one another's life, including every little detail there was to know. He opened the book of his life in front of me and let me read it word by word. However, I wasn't as brave as he was, so when my turn came to share my secrets, I had to tear some pages from my life book; I just didn't have the courage to share it all. As much as I wanted to tell him everything about my brother and my past, something inside of me stopped me. The fear that things might blow out of proportion and I may end up losing him never let me open up.

Keeping that one thing away from him affected me, but I tried not to think about it. I focused on the present and worked for the betterment of the future, which was linked with Andy. It wasn't hard to stay in the moment with him and get to know him more. Everything was so easy around him. We could talk for hours, and still, it would feel like seconds. He was indeed the most magical thing that had ever happened to me.

Those weeks of getting to know him were the best. It felt surreal and too good to be true. I kept pinching myself to ensure that it was all a reality. Everything was falling into place, and all the gloominess in my life was slowly fading away.

Finally, I had someone to call mine and be possessive about. It was an exciting and equally challenging part to get to know each other. It was easy, but the unsaid complexity tried to hijack the delicacy of our connection. Sometimes, those deranged emotions and flashbacks from the past tried to destroy what I had with him, but I never allowed any of those feelings to take over. I trusted him more than anything and never wanted to let anyone or anything take that away from me.

Going to church together and sharing what we wanted for each other in the future and for us as a couple was the most wholesome feeling. Time somehow picked pace, and without me realizing it, I turned 16. The sixteenth year of my life was filled with sweetness, and I had someone to call mine. Just looking into his eyes solved half of my problems, and I couldn't have asked for more. We both respected each other and our bond and the respect I had for him doubled after we went on the first date.

I finally went out on a date with him when I turned 16. After winding up our cute little date, he closed his eyes to say a prayer to the Almighty. In that prayer, he thanked God for allowing him to meet this incredible girl. I could feel my cheeks burning, and a wave of joy coursed through me. Not only was I the happiest, but also the luckiest person that I got to meet this amazing person. All my life, I wanted to serve the purpose of God and lead a life as per His teachings. Luckily, I found someone who was equally devoted to God, and it was like a dream come true. Now, there was no way that I was going to let this beautiful thing go.

He was the most loving, considerate, and caring man I have ever met. In just a short span of time, he had showered a significant amount of love toward me, something I lacked in my life.

It all worked so beautifully because of our chemistry and belief system. Our lives were all settled around God, and living and serving him was the main motto of it. I feel our faith and trust in God also played an important role in our relationship. It made us more respectful toward one another and filled our hearts with adoration and pure love.

***

Within no time, Mom and I found ourselves completely involved in the matters of the Church. My mother started attending the Ladies' meetings once a month, and some of these women became really good friends with Mom, and they also started visiting our house. Witnessing my mother settling in and finally moving on was oddly satisfying. Mom needed that since she was a widow, and for the first time since Dad had passed away, she was able to make some friends. It all created a positive impact on her life.

My mother was 44 when she went forward to accept Jesus as her savior. It brought out a really good change in her, and I was pretty happy with her decision. It enabled her to grow her wings in a positive direction without letting it hurt her. And now, her behavior and treatment toward me had changed as well. We had a great, loving mother-daughter relationship now, and I didn't want to jinx it.

In June of 1967, the church had a revival for the first time and had Rev. Jack Baskins as the guest speaker. He had been a Missionary to Korea since 1959. Since he was such a big personality, everyone was quite excited to see him – including me.

When he visited the church, everyone was with him for a while, and I did the same as well. I initiated this by introducing myself to him, and we hit it off quickly because his wife's name was the same as mine. During that short meeting, we became friends and started spending time with each other. He talked to me every day, and we both had so much in common. He also had a daughter about my age, so he said it was easy for him to understand my perspective and relate to it.

After that week, on Sunday morning, I went to accept Jesus as my personal Savior. Apparently, it was also Father's Day, and I was doing it for my father as well. I went forward to take Jesus as my Savior, and I prayed to God to help me, guide me, direct me, and protect me the way no one ever had.

Directing myself more toward God helped me in ways that I could never explain. Now I knew that God had His blessings on me and He would never leave me alone. Moving forward in life under the guidance provided by God was quite easy. He was making a path for me and was helping me miraculously with every twist and turn in life. I had complete faith in the Almighty, and I knew that I would never be alone again.

***

One of the nights, after the church dinner, I had a conversation with Rev. Baskins. He talked to me about serving God more and becoming a missionary myself. I felt honored because it was something enormous. The best part was he felt I could do it. I was smiling as I answered him, "I will surely do it if that is the Lord's will for my life."

He also said he would keep in touch with me and help me in any way possible. He also told me about the Bible College in Springfield, Mo., where a lot of Preachers go and collect insightful information about the religion. Every year, this college also conducts a week of meetings during the month of May, right before graduation. He suggested I visit this college and consider becoming a part of it. There was a solitude on his face as he concluded, "It will be a good, new spiritual experience for you. You will be able to do something for yourself and for God. And that's not it; you will be able to heal your mind and body."

I said I would think about it. Then, in June, I decided to accept his advice and follow the path of God. Undoubtedly, it was a great experience. I was able to connect with the inner self.

Days after I gave my life to Jesus, Andy stepped ahead and directed his life toward God. Right when he got out of the Air Force, he felt the Lord was calling him to become a Pastor. At that point, our relationship was going quite strong, and we were pretty serious about one another – marriage was on the list, too.

So, Andy talked to me about it and explained how he felt God was calling him to align his body and soul with His purpose for life and become a pastor. It made me the happiest person on the planet. I couldn't contain my excitement and seconded with those visions. I advised him to take those hints and follow that trail. Then, he let it all in the hands of God and followed His lead, and God helped him sail through.

"Many are the plans in a person's heart, but it is the LORD's purpose that prevails."

-*Proverbs 19:21*

Chapter 5: Andy

LOVE is just a small, four-letter word, but it encompasses a broad term, almost like collecting the entire universe. It is a sacred emotion that can never be expressed in words and has to be felt. It has the power to change the magnitude of your life. When you are in love, you can hear it in quietness and even see it with the lights out. All of a sudden, everything will feel different. That's how Shirley's life was colored in bright shades, and she felt butterflies in her stomach. The flush on her cheeks was evident at all times, and the reason behind her electric smile was her knight in shining armor, her lifesaver – Andy.

Andy was raised in a Baptist church in Roxbury, Mass. His family lived with one of his uncles, who owned a quarter portion of a small house around the church's property. He devoted most of his life to doing the maintenance work in the church, and that's how he was given this property. Andy's uncle was also one of the ushers, just like his father.

Andy's oldest sister married a wonderful man right after she graduated from high school. His name was Fred, and he was a great influence on Andy. Fred was the one who always gave Andy career advice and counseled him to join the Air Force. He said it would be like living a dream he never had the chance to live. Fred had joined the army in his youth, but he collapsed during the training program in Texas. He was hospitalized and stayed unconscious for a while. Then, he was diagnosed with diabetes, which took everyone by surprise. So, it put a halt to his career in the military, and he had to bid a sad goodbye to his dream of being in the army. That's why he wanted to live his dream through Andy.

Andy always did everything for his family, so he agreed and asked for his parents' approval. Everyone felt proud of his decision and supported him entirely. During this duration, Andy was building a stronger connection with God, and with the promise to serve the Lord and humanity to the best of his ability, he joined the Air Force on August 1, 1966.

In the beginning, he was given basic training in Texas and an additional six weeks in the printing press room. After being trained, Andy was chosen for Top Secret Clearance in the printing shop. He was the only one selected from his base, making him feel on top of the world. He justified his selection and gave his best performance.

Time passed quickly, and within three months, Andy was stationed at Shepperd Air Force Base in the town where Mom and I Lived. His roommate was the son of a preacher, and they both got along pretty well.

After settling on the base, they both started coming to the same church I attended. The Pastor himself had been in the Air Force, so he always welcomed Airmen with great hospitality. Every Sunday afternoon, all the families around the church would feed those Airmen with delicious homemade meals. It was overwhelming for Andy to witness such warmth and generosity, and he enjoyed it all to the core.

Andy's close interest in the religion and his curiosity to know more made him grow closer to the Pastor, and they became great friends. While serving humankind and God around the church,

Andy had this sudden revelation to do something more for his Lord. He felt something was missing, and a voice called out to him, and he surrendered to become a Pastor.

By that time, Andy and I were in a relationship. We were both immensely in love, and he was undoubtedly the best man on the planet. He supported me in every decision, and now it was my time to show him some support. I backed him up on that decision and stood by his side throughout.

Andy learned a lot as he stepped on this journey to become a pastor. He spent several hours every week with our Pastor, who taught him many of the ins and outs of this spiritual voyage. Andy was always a keen learner and paid attention to everything demonstrated to him. He even took notes and implemented that stated point in the next lesson. It was why he was liked and respected by many preachers he met over the years. His devoted and kind nature had also blessed him with many companions. They all helped, taught, and prayed for him all the time.

***

When I decided to walk on the path of light and follow God, it brought a miraculous change in my life. It got me closer to my religion and helped me find the man of my dreams. He got into my life as an angel and guided me in every walk of life. Andy was literally like a magnet that pulled me out of the darkness. He pushed me beyond my limits and always asked me to believe completely in God. That's how I sailed through this journey and started living my life for Jesus.

It strengthened my relationship with Andy. We weren't just good friends anymore; we were soulmates, and every time we both worked on a project together, our bond deepened. He was the one to inject me with all the positivity and ask me to keep moving. Ever since I was little, I never had enough confidence in myself. I felt I was flawed and lacked something. Thanks to Andy, he boosted my self-esteem and showed me how to feel protected and comfortable in my own skin.

He made me plant a garden of memories with him, and some of them will stay with me forever. Thinking about all those beautiful flashbacks always took me back to when I was in high school. While I was in high school, our youth group would arrange a get-together with students from other churches. Every month, all of us would go to another church group close by, about 50 miles from our church. I always took part in several games and contests. It was like a little getaway to detoxify our minds.

There, we had Bible drills where the pastor would read a verse, and we had to guess the scripture. Whoever did it first scored a point. Then, there were verse explanations, memorization of verses, and so much more. So, that's how the entire day was spent there, and then we ended our days with some tasty food and sundaes.

During the summer, when Andy got to be a part of our church group, he was introduced to these youth groups. By that time, we were kind of serious about one another. So, when he started going to that event, he usually did Bible drills. Usually, we both participated in the same games and won most of them. Later on, instead of participating, we started organizing those youth camps.

As time progressed, we got to be a big part of those youth camps. I could never forget when we were working with the teens in the youth groups. He'd keep glancing at me while we worked, and when our eyes would meet, we would smile at each other. It was pure love, the kind that I had never shared with anyone else in my life. It was like I had been blessed with all the love and adoration I lacked as a child. All of my wishes came true through him, and I will always be thankful to him for making me feel this special.

***

They all say high school romances don't always last. But Andy and I both were here to prove them wrong. With every passing hour, my love for him kept increasing. He never gave me a chance to unlove or dislike him because he was everything I wanted and needed. He was a listener, a helper, a mentor, a lover, and most importantly, a good friend. I could talk to him about anything and can be totally myself. So, there was no way that I was letting it all ever go.

The starting phase of every relationship is filled with dates. There is always the first spot where it all starts, and then the billing receipts keep naming different restaurants and cafes as you spend more time together. Similarly, Andy and I both went on a lot of dates. That time was full of joy and laughter. I still recall how we went outside for dinner for the first time. I was nervous and shy, but I couldn't stop blushing. He was smiling at me too - but not in the way of making fun, instead to make you know that you are the prettiest girl in the room. His personality was really soothing, and his comforting nature booked an apartment of his name in my heart. I instantly knew, "HE IS THE ONE."

There was this drive down around the main street that sold the best burgers in town. We went there a lot of times to help our cravings. We also went on dates at McDonald's, Burger King, Wendy's, Dairy Queen, Sonic, Pizza Hut, and Griff's Burger, which was our favorite.

Griff's Burger was a really big burger joint in our vicinity. It was our signature pit stop station that we visited every Friday night. We always ordered their best burger, fries, and coke, and I'd have the best things in front of me – one was the food, and the other was none other than Andy.

I also want to mention one of my best dates with him. I was really into cinema and was a fan of good plot and direction. So, a movie named Dr. Zhivago had just come out. Andy got free from the base that day and suggested watching that movie together in the cinema.

When we went to the air base's only theater, they weren't playing the movie we wanted to watch. Instead, they were having the next show for The Blob, which was about to start in twenty minutes. The Blob had Steve McQueen in it, and he was a terrific actor. So, we decided to watch that movie as the poster seemed quite appealing too.

The Blob had quite a good plot, and Andy was amazed by the action sequences in the movie. He wouldn't stop talking about its high level of acting and how it was shot. Those were like great 160 minutes, and we enjoyed every second of it. However, I jumped from the seat during several scenes and grabbed Andy's hand a little too tight whenever a scary scene came on. He would laugh first but then caress my shoulder and hold my hand. The way he protected me always felt unreal.

After finishing the movie, we did the usual and went to Griff's again and filled out tummies with their extra saucy burgers. It was indeed a night to remember.

Other than eating out, Andy also visited our home and enjoyed the homemade food as well. He was pretty grounded and low maintenance, and those worldly things never mattered to him. He always found pleasure in those little things and appreciated the beauty of life. So, whenever he was home, my mother would cook a fancy dish he liked. After eating, we would always play a game of dominoes together or watch a movie.

Both of our parents knew about us and were really supportive of our relationship. Andy had already met my family several times, and now it was time for me to meet his family. My heart was racing like a fast car on a track, and I was anxious. In my defense, I was just a seventeen-year-old who was madly in love and wanted her boyfriend's parents to like her.

Andy was on leave, and he had left town to meet his folks. After going there, he thought that I should meet his parents, and called me, asking me to come. I was resistant because it felt too much too fast. So, I tried my best to stall, but he made his mother call me. Andy's entire family was soft-spoken, and she had a way with words. You couldn't say 'no' to her.

Andy's mother called and asked if I would like to come to meet them. I paused as I didn't know what to say. Then, she further added, "Andy talks about you all the time. It would be a pleasure to meet you! Also, I am sending you the tickets as well, so don't worry about it."

It was kind of cute, and nobody had ever done that for me. I felt really special at that moment, and my heart was filled with happiness. "You didn't have to do that," I was being formal, but she cut me down and, in her melodious voice, said, "Andy is my child, and so are you! So, be here; we all will wait."

It was hard to convince my mother, but she came around. I was frightened when I reached out because I didn't know what would happen, but Andy smoothened the entire process. His family welcomed me warmly, and then Andy introduced me to everyone. His house was filled with people that day, and Andy made me talk to his relatives and immediate family members. Then, as the clock rang eight, Andy took my hand, made me walk toward the center of the living room, and got down on his one knee. Then he took a ring out and asked, "Would you like to put a label on me and call me yours forever?"

It was too cliché, but it did the deed for me. I couldn't believe it was finally happening. The air felt odd, and I could feel the warmth on my skin. I was not expecting it at all, but I was the happiest. Tears of happiness dripped down my eyes as I shouted, "YES!! YESS!!! YESSS!!!! A MILLION TIMES, YES!!!!!"

He slid the ring on my finger and then stood up, hugging me. It was undoubtedly the happiest day of my life. I wanted to scream at the top of my lungs and tell the world about this victory of love.

***

Putting the label of marriage on relationships is never easy. A person must be certain before taking such a big step, and I had complete confidence in my love for Andy and his affection for me. We were like a match made in heaven. Though, initially, I had no plans to get married, when he told me about pursuing his education in religion, I couldn't stop myself. Right in that second, my respect for him doubled, and I wanted to show all my affection toward him. So, when he finally kneeled and asked me to marry him in April of that year before going to college, I instantly shouted, "YES."

It was quite hard to believe because I wasn't only marrying the person that I loved but also the person who was my biggest supporter and dear friend. It was like a union of love, where we turned from best friends to family. He was four years older than me. I was 18 when we got married. Since then, I have called myself a proud wife of that man.

When we tied the knot, we started college within two months. We were together all the time, from attending classes to getting to know each other in the early months of marriage.

Since we were a couple, we moved into the married couple's dorm. It was right across the main campus. There were two buildings, three stories each, with around 72 apartments in total. All of them were quite furbished and had a sofa, kitchen table along with four chairs, one coffee table and a small chair, a stove, and a refrigerator. So, it was a decent place to live.

We lived in the building facing the campus, and we could see it through the window. Other than a peaceful view, we also had pretty good neighbors. Often, the four couples on our floor would have dinner together, each bringing some to add to the others. We usually have the best party once a month.

Right before enrolling for the second year, I had surgery, so I couldn't go to college. I couldn't do many house chores because I was advised not to do them for a little while. Hence, Andy was always the one to help me in that compartment, and sometimes, the neighbor would also offer their assistance, which I appreciated. However, I got better with time, and I started caring for the apartment on my own.

Andy had been a man of many talents. He never wanted his family to go through a hard time, so he did everything he could to provide them with a good lifestyle. Since we were now a family, he took a cleaning job to ensure we met our needs. While he was working there, I was mostly at home preparing notes from the books and research so he could study from it.

After the first year of college, we had good news to cherish. I was expecting, and we couldn't contain this excitement. He was happy, and I was thrilled. Once the initial excitement of the new subsided, we realized that our responsibilities would increase with the baby's arrival. Now, the duties were not just tripled but quadrupled, and he had to get on some extra work to earn more. Since I had to rest, I was home more than most of the time, so I utilized it to create notes for Andy.

Due to the extra work, Andy had to work late on some nights, and then he would study until midnight. It would be really chaotic during the days of exams, as he had a lot of points to cover in very little time.

Unfortunately, within just two months of pregnancy, I had a miscarriage. My world was trembling, and I couldn't do anything to save it. Andy was equally sad, but he never showed it. He always put up a strong front, hiding his emotions to give me strength. It was healing, but it was a long and slow process. I mean, losing a baby is like death by a thousand cuts. I was physically weak, emotionally drenched, and unable to attend classes. So, I had no other option but to skip those. However, Andy stood there like a rock, supporting and loving me no matter what.

It was hard, but God helped clear out the dark clouds. He heard our miseries and cries and blessed me in ways I couldn't explain. After two years, Andy graduated, and I was expecting another child, which the doctor said was a miracle because when I lost the baby, they said I could never get pregnant again. It was really big news; I was extra careful and prayed for a healthy delivery. And this time, all of those prayers were heard. We were blessed with a beautiful baby girl, and 18 months later, we had a healthy little boy. When I held my babies for the first time, everything stopped, and their little coo was all that remained. My life was magically changed that day. I was a mother now...

Chapter 6: Graduation

In 1965, Andy graduated from Boston Technical High School in Boston, Mass. Then, in 1966, he joined the Air Force Base and went to Lackland Air Force Base in San Antonio, Texas. He did some basic training there and continued using the multilift press as he did in high school. Andy served in the military for four years and was a part of the Sheppard Air Force Base during the Vietnam War.

On the contrary, I graduated from high school in 1970. We didn't host a big party or celebrate extensively for my graduation because Andy and I were getting married in just two weeks. So, instead of making my graduation a big event, we started preparing for the wedding. But I did go out for dinner with my mom and Andy after graduation.

My wedding preparations were going in full swing. I had already bought the material for my dress and got it stitched by a friend's mother. This friend was also my maid of honor, and her name was Carol. She was more excited than me and kept me updated about the dress. Once her mother was done with it, she called me in for a fitting. I was glad to see how elegant I looked when I put it on. The dress was satin white, and the front panel and the sleeves were embellished with lace. To say that I was mesmerized after trying it on would not be a lie. Even Carol complimented me and told me I looked stunning. However, it did require a few adjustments, but her mother said she would do it all in a day.

Carol was like my sister; we had been best friends ever since I could remember. That's why her mother agreed to make the dress for me. I still remember the old days when I started going to church and met her for the first time. It was an instant connection, and our friendship brewed instantly and grew organically over time. Then, when Andy got in the picture, all three of us started hanging out with each other. There were a lot of times when Andy and I had dinner at her place and stayed late, watching movies or playing games. Sometimes, we also used to pick her up and take her out for dinner. We even participated in all the church activities together. That was a great time.

Even if I take it back to the summers, Carol and I spent most of our time with each other. Then, every Friday, there was a sleepover, and I would stay at her place, or she would come over. We even went on double dates and introduced our boyfriends to each other. It was like sibling love, and I could never let go of it. Even to this day, I feel lucky to be still connected with her because she was a diamond that I could never lose.

With Carol as my maid of honor, I also had another friend as a bridesmaid. Both wore a pink dress with a floral panel on the front and sleeves. It also had pink ribbon covering the edges of the flowers, giving them a more polished look. Sadly, the other friend who was my bridesmaid couldn't attend the wedding and had to go out of town urgently. She was married to a military guy who was stationed in Vietnam. He was allowed to take his leave for rest and recovery and visit Hawaii for a week. As he was going there, his wife needed to be there too, so she had to leave to be with her husband. And being very honest, knowing what it feels like to spend time with your loved ones, I didn't mind it at all. She was doing it for the person she loved and the person she got married to. Hence, she had all the right to do it and was really happy with her decision. So, it was just Carol and me who were ready to do all the 'Maid of Honor' duties.

Most of the preparations were almost finished by the time I graduated from high school. But some things still needed my assistance, so I did them one by one. After the trial of my wedding dress, I went to a flower shop to order the flowers for the event. I have always loved white roses, and I believe they are the best flowers to exist. My wedding wouldn't be completed without them, so I ordered a bouquet of white roses for myself. For Carol, I ordered a bouquet of pink roses and got more flowers for the reception table. The design that I had in mind revolved around flowers. I wanted the stage to be filled with white roses intertwined around the candles on the Cadillac candelabra. I also wanted two big sets of white and pink roses on both sides of the pulpit. So, I ordered the flowers in bulk to ensure everything was set up properly.

By then, I had already been to the bakery and chosen my wedding cake. It was a three-tier cake with roses descending in a spiral from top to bottom. It also had a bride and groom sitting on the top. It was one of the best cakes that Margie's bakery had to offer, and so I jumped on the opportunity to get it immediately. I have been a loyal customer of this bakery since I got to know about it. Ever since Margie, the owner, started visiting church and became a friend, I couldn't stop visiting her bakery shop and trying out all the amazing stuff there. Everything that it had to offer tasted like heaven. Hence, I knew I could trust Margie's baking skills for my wedding.

It was Michael, Margie's grandson, who became the owner after Margie's death, who made the cake, but Margie and his mother baked it. Undoubtedly, it looked great, and we had to arrange it at the church on the wedding day. We also set up two tables in the activity room and placed a tablecloth on both. There was also a bowl of mints, almonds, and the cake on one table. In contrast, the other table had all the cups and punch bowls.

Back in 1970, there wasn't a fancy dinner like people have in modern times. Instead, there was just punch, cake, and some other sweet delights, like the mints and almonds we had. At my wedding, Carol's mother, with one of my aunts on her mother's side, served the cake while Andy's older sister, Janet, served the punch.

Although we didn't do anything lavish, and the wedding was simple and small, I still had a lot of fun. It was a very nice and calm ceremony, and everyone who attended had a great time. It was fun to see people celebrating us and enjoying the company.

While Andy's older sister attended to the guests and served them, his younger sister sang at the wedding. She sang a song for us and did a commendable job. Everyone applauded and praised her. After that, she sang a prayer song. Andy and I kneeled at the prayer bench as she sang a hymn for us in her magical voice. I ordered it from the flower shop, and it was blossoming with scents of different flowers as we prayed.

Andy and I went to the hotel room we had booked as we finished all the rituals. We couldn't go to Andy's house because his family stayed there and the whole house was occupied. So, to get some privacy, we got ourselves a hotel room and spent some alone time there – just the two of us, free from the chaos of the world.

Andy's parents stayed with us for another week. We had a great time with them, and then they flew home. After that, it was just Andy and I left, and we stayed at his apartment until he got out of service. Then, we drove to Massachusetts. His parents threw a reception there and invited some close friends and family.

***

Andy had two brothers, but he was closest to the youngest one. His name was Jimmy, and he always believed in doing things his way. Although he had a mind of his own and never liked interference, Jimmy always valued his opinions when it came to Andy.

After our marriage, our time in Massachusetts turned out to be quite fun. Andy and I used to go on double dates with Jimmy and his girlfriend. Jimmy was a mind-blowing bowler. So, a couple of times, we also went to the bowling alley. Although I wasn't very good at it, it didn't stop me from trying my best.

But we were only able to go out on a few double dates, as Jimmy broke up with his girlfriend. They were going through some issues and had to call it off because it wasn't working out between them. Soon after that, Jimmy met somebody else, and they clicked off instantly. She worked at the Museum of Fine Arts.

Carol and I turned into sisters-in-law after she married Jimmy. They both loved each other dearly and became parents to three children. Their daughter was born in the same year as my son. He was born in March, and their daughter was born in October, so it was just a few months' difference. Unfortunately, Lori, as a young woman, passed away suddenly. She had a brain aneurysm, and it took her life.

The whole family was left devastated after her death, affecting Jimmy the most. He didn't express it, but he was suffocating inside because it was his only daughter. Jimmy and I got close, too, and after a tragic loss in my life, he was there to support me. He and Carol were always there to support me, and they helped me regain stability.

***

After finishing four years in the Air Force, Andy was given an honorable discharge from the military. He was applauded for his services, and everyone had nice things to say about him. Afterward, we packed and left for a little trip before heading to college.

We left Wichita with some essential items like clothes and crockery. It was a long journey, and we took several stops. Our first destination was Massachusetts, where we stopped the car for some sightseeing. We spent some time at a peaceful café and then went to a glass store to buy fancy glasses. We thought having these types of glasses for our house would be cool. I liked all of them, so we went with Andy's choice and bought four glasses from that factory.

From there, we went on a tour of Goodyear Tire Co. Andy was always enthusiastic about such things, and he convinced me to go there. I thought it would be boring, but going there changed my mind. It was a brand-new experience, and I really liked it.

It was pretty serene driving toward Boston. The building shone brightly against the traffic-studded roads. We spent two weeks touring that place. We went to Bunker Hill, Old North Church, The Coast of the Ocean, the State House Building, Boston Gardens, and the place where Paul Revere was buried. Those places were great, and we had an amazing time exploring them. We also shopped from the most famous Boston – Faneuil Hall marketplace market.

While in Boston, we also took a trip down to the old houses where early patriotists lived. We learned about their old culture and way of living. We also explored the Salem witches and Southie, where the Italians lived, and from there, we went to Dorchester and Roxbury. It was the place where Andy was born and raised. He showed me around, but nothing was the same as it used to be. He kept telling me how it was all different in his time and how it progressed.

On the first Saturday that we were there, Andy's mom and dad told us that they had organized a small reception for us. It was held in a meeting room in one of the banks, and I loved the setting. Everything was in place, and the setup looked great. Everyone was excited to see us as we arrived and came rushing to meet and greet us.

I didn't know anyone, so Andy's mom and dad introduced me to everyone there. Everyone was welcoming and nice, making me feel like I belonged. I met Andy's uncles, aunts, cousins, friends, and neighbors, and it was fun to know some of them. His two best friends (Marco and Petersen) from school were also there. They also met me and introduced themselves.

I was noticeably different, and it wasn't hard to guess that I was a girl from Texas. My accent was speaking volumes. At the same time, they all had very different accents, and we laughed about it. Then, I sarcastically told them how I said "YES!" to Andy without knowing what he had asked me. It was obviously a pun because I was just being witty. I could never forget what he said when he proposed to me. Everyone started laughing after that.

In that reception, everything was the best. The parents got us a customized cake, and it felt like we were again doing all the wedding rituals. Other than the cake, they had sandwiches and other eating items. There was also an open bar, but we didn't go there because we never drank.

We also got a lot of gifts from the guests, but mostly everyone gave us money. It was because Andy's parents had asked everyone to give us money as we traveled and then had to soon structure our lives in a new place. I was blown away by their hospitality, and it indeed marked a night to remember.

The Tuesday after the reception was quite happening as well. Andy and I went to the Museum of Fine Arts in the afternoon. That's where most of Andy's family had worked in the past. It was a historic place to visit, and Andy had a lot to talk about, and I was all ears.

This Museum of Fine Arts in Boston is one of the most famous museums in the world. Not only was it around the most luxurious location, but it also had the greatest views. That museum also had some very prestigious portraits and paintings that add more value to this momentous place's beauty.

Every Tuesday night, the dining area of the museum was opened for dinner, and everyone was allowed to join the feast. Andy's mother also worked in the restaurant every Tuesday night. Jimmy, Andy's brother and one of Andy's dad's sisters, worked as a cook at the Museum of Fine Arts. Edna, Andy's aunt, was head chef at the restaurant for several years, and her children also worked at the museum. Now, as we were there, and Andy had been an integral part of the museum in the past, we were asked to be the dining room manager for that night.

Since one of the girls didn't show up for work, her responsibility landed on my shoulders. Now, I had to be the night waitress and was told I would be given two tables to work. So, without any hesitation, I agreed. On the other hand, Andy's job was to clean the tables and set them up for the next customers.

We both always made a good team, and we were also quite exceptional at this new job. Although it was just a two-hour gig, we gave it our best. I was told I would serve two tables, but I was working six tables by the night's end. I still didn't complain and did everything within my capacity. Similarly, Andy helped everyone else out of his duties and ensured that everything was happening systematically.

Initially, we were told we would be given 75 dollars for two hours, but we were shocked when we got paid. It was a great surprise because we got double what we expected. Instead of getting 75 dollars for two hours, we got 150, i.e., 75 for each hour. Other than that, I had 340$ tips, so it credited a great amount in our pockets. Despite getting a good amount, all of us had a great time. It made me learn so many things, and I was able to channel the hidden skills within me that I never knew existed.

It brought a new energetic stride within me, and I would cherish it forever.

When we traveled back to the college, we were completely different people. Both of us learned a lot from this trip, and it allowed us to explore ourselves individually. But the one thing that didn't change at all was our love and adoration for each other. This little journey made us grow closer and strengthened our bond more.

Chapter 7: Bible College

It's true what they say about how contagious laughter is. But guess what? I believe that love is too - not in a loud, boisterous way but rather in a steady, quiet manner that originates from a lifetime of dedication. That's how things were between Andy and I. He was like a big tree, providing me with shade and support. And under his affection and protection, I was growing freely. He completed me, and I made life easy for him.

When we got together, it was like a union of togetherness where we were enough for each other. After experiencing that kind of love, it was impossible to picture living without it. Now, though, the responsibilities had gotten bigger after marriage; there was laundry to do, bills to pay, and a future to build, but under the mundane routine, the love was still there - warm, snug, and just as real as it was in the beginning.

After we got married, we went to Massachusetts for a month to have another reception. It was like a holiday spree where we enjoyed the vacations and explored Massachusetts's culture as a couple. It was a great experience to visit a place where Andy spent his entire childhood. He loved showing me around and telling me the things he did as a kid. It made me fall in love with him more, and I felt honored to be included.

Our marriage was held in a small ceremony in Texas, followed by the reception there, and consisted mostly of my family and friends. Since Andy's family lived around Massachusetts, his parents gave us a reception once we visited them. So, it was now time for a grand event.

Everything about the reception was magnificent, and his family and friends were all very welcoming. Andy introduced me to everyone, and it was good to know them. Since we were going to live on our own soon and start college, Andy's mother suggested that everyone give us money instead of gifts. It was very thoughtful of her because, unlike gifts, we could use that money for books, food, car maintenance, and any other bills.

Andy's mother was the sweetest, but at the same time, she was a formidable woman, and everyone did what she said. She had that personality that left you with no other option but to listen to her. That's why it wasn't easy to say no to her. This time was no different, and everyone agreed to her suggestion and obeyed it (They were scared to say no, ha-ha.)

After the reception, we counted the money we received after all the guests were gone. It was just me and Andy in the room, and we were surprised by the hefty amount we had collected. We received around $2800, which we couldn't believe it. Back in 1970, it was considered a lot. Neither Andy nor I expected that we would return loaded from there. All thanks to his mother, who was so considerate about our future.

But this wasn't the only money we earned during our stay in Massachusetts. When we were there one evening, we also worked at the Museum of Fine Arts Restaurant along with Andy's family. They were short on staff, and we tagged along to offer them extra help. We both did our parts with extreme honesty. That honesty paid off, and we both made around $490 in just two hours, including tips. It was almost unbelievable, but I was happy that we wouldn't be moving to college with a low bank balance.

***

Andy and I started freshman year at Bible College, taking the Missions course because we were uncertain where to head. We weren't sure what the Lord was calling us to do, so we went with the Missions course, thinking it would either lead to us becoming missionaries or, in Andy's case, a pastor.

We attended most of the classes together, and it was quite fun throughout the first semester. However, I had to have an operation in the second year, and because of this, I couldn't attend classes for a while. My condition was severe, and I was told I probably wouldn't be able to have kids.

Since I was completely bedridden and couldn't attend any classes, Andy decided to pursue his dream of becoming a pastor. He dropped the Missions course and went ahead on this new journey. Along with his studies, he also worked 40 hours per week doing commercial cleaning, which he did for many years. He had his own company that did commercial cleaning. Andy even employed 13 church members in his company. However, this never interfered with his church work over the years.

All that time, when he was juggling between work and school, I decided to make his studies a bit easier for him. I was home mostly, so I utilized this time productively by doing the research work for his papers. He was supposed to work on different research papers for the course, and I helped him with that. I dug out as much information as possible and wrote it all down in a notebook so he could use it all later.

Since Andy had a really tight schedule, he didn't have much time to read. He always read the research the night before the paper was due, and that's where I came to the rescue. He would come home from work, skim through the notes I prepared, work on research, and ace the exams. Sometimes, some work was due, and he forgot to complete it. He would come home and immediately go to sleep. Hence, to give him those few hours of rest, I often typed the rest of the pages and did the work that was left. So, a contributive effort of both enabled him to flourish in this journey.

We lived on campus, and it was a short walk to go to the main building for classes. There were two buildings, one for married couples and the other one for couples who had a kid too. We lived in the part of the building that was designated for married people only.

We lived on the third floor. Since our side of the building had four apartments, four different couples lived there, including us. We all bonded well, and usually, once a month, we would combine our food and would eat together. We used to do it around the small outdoor sitting area. It was inside both the buildings and had a small grill as well. So, we would cook, bring our food there, and then enjoy the lovely evening with each other's company and the tasty food, obviously.

The apartments were small but efficient, with a Murphy bed that folded out of the wall. However, due to my medical condition, it was sometimes a hassle to sleep on that Murphy bed. Then, pulling it out and then pushing it back in often triggered stomach pain. But I managed it quite well and learned to live in that situation.

My stomach pain had a long history. I started feeling pain in my stomach when I was 12 years old. Shortly after my dad passed away, my condition worsened, and the stomach pain got a lot more intense, so much so that I had to go through surgery. I was just 12 but had cysts on my ovaries, which caused a lot of pain and operations over the next few years.

Cysts around ovaries are basically the formation of sacs that are filled with fluid. Over time, they can get bigger and, if not treated, can cause infertility in females. That's what happened to me, too, according to the doctors, at least.

In that phase, I used to get heavy pelvic pain. I used to feel very full even after eating a little. It led to these regular medical treatments – one after another. I first had surgery at 12, then another major one at 16. Unfortunately, the pain didn't get any better and kept worsening with time, which was what led to another surgery in my second year at college.

The pain was still there even after all those surgeries. It also affected my menstruation period, which was always bad, with a lot of bleeding and pain.

***

Between my first and second years of college, Andy and I went to Kansas, where he worked for a pastor during the summer. We had known this pastor for quite a while by then, and Andy felt privileged to work under him. It was also a great learning opportunity for him, and he was excited about the Church.

While working for him, Andy helped clean and manage the hospital visits. He also would cater to the new visitors and welcome them into the church. Then, he also drove the bus to pick up people who needed a ride to the church. At that time, I was the secretary, and we both worked together as a unit to live the dream we shared.

During that phase, I started having awful pain in my stomach. It was so bad that I couldn't even sit properly. So, the assistant pastor's wife took me to her doctor. That doctor suggested I go to the hospital because, after a detailed examination, he felt my right ovary was enlarged.

We listened to the doctor, and I was taken to the hospital immediately. I was hospitalized for a while and had to recuperate for a few weeks. After that, we decided to go back to my hometown, where I could stay with my mother after the surgery. For the time being, I planned to live with my mother while Andy finished college. Then, when I could travel again, I would join Andy.

In the first surgery, my right ovary, tube, and a part of my intestines were removed. They were completely infected with endometriosis, so they had to be removed permanently. Furthermore, I was informed that it would be hard for me to have children if it wasn't impossible.

Andy was there with me during the surgery and stayed with me for a while after. When I got discharged and returned home, there was nothing to wear because everything was back at my college dorm. Sadly, we didn't bring anything with us, so then my mother had to arrange clothes for both of us.

On the first night after the surgery, I was in a devastating state of discomfort. It was a weird kind of pain that was fading in and out. I was in bed, resting, but my face was expressing the pain I was going through. Then, I started sobbing, which quickly escalated into an ugly cry. I wanted to stop the tears, but I couldn't. They just kept dripping, one after another.

Witnessing that, Andy curled up in bed and lay next to me. Then he dabbed my tears and soaked them dry. He asked if I was hurting.

"Yeah, a little, but there's a lot going on in my head," I replied.

"What's that?" he asked.

I looked him in the eyes and whispered, "I don't know where this will go. I probably won't get better and won't be able to give you kids. It isn't fair to you. So, I think we should divorce, and you should marry someone else. From my side, you are allowed to and deserve it." A tear rolled down my cheek.

The doctors had told me multiple times that I might not be able to get pregnant. This just kept repeating in my mind over and over again. I knew Andy loved kids, so I didn't want to rob him of that happiness.

"Shut up! Never say anything like that again." He was adamant.

Andy continued, "I married you because I love you - not for what you can do for me or give me."

"But I..." I was about to say something, but he didn't let me conclude and stopped me. "As I said, discussion closed." That was the last time the topic of divorce was ever mentioned, and then we never discussed it again.

Andy was the only one who could ever tell me to shut up, and it wouldn't make me mad; instead, it would calm me down. After that heated discussion, he took me in his arms, and we quietly lay in bed together for over an hour. I fell asleep in the same position.

While I was sleeping, Andy helped Mom with dinner and some other work. He made his special spaghetti with meat sauce, probably the only thing he could cook. Then he cleaned up everything after we were done eating. He was a special man - one in a million, and everyone loved him. I consider myself extremely lucky that he fell in love with me.

He was the best thing that had ever happened to me and the best part of the two of us in our marriage. He was caring, affectionate, and kind, and he never stopped amazing me with his warmth and adoration. I was so lucky to be called his wife.

Chapter 8: Salvation and Called to Preach

The saddest reality of existence is unpredictability. You can never foresee what's going to happen next, nor can you go into the past to change anything. That's what makes it a bit difficult to find balance in this slippery slope of life when you don't even know if you are going to make it to the next morning, let alone predict what life will have to offer you in the next few months. That's why we are advised to live to the fullest; we don't know what is going to happen next, and we don't know if we will be alive or not. Andy had also lost his dear brother-in-law in a pretty similar way. He was there, all fine and well, and then suddenly, he was gone, just like that, and we couldn't do anything.

Andy was really close to his brother-in-law, who was married to his older sister. Besides being a great human being, Andy had learned so much under his guidance. The best thing about him was that he made everything so smooth sailing for Andy, and he didn't have a hard time practicing his relationship with God anymore. His name was Fred, and he was undoubtedly a great Christian influence in Andy's life to become closer and grow fond of his religion more profoundly.

Unexpectedly, Fred died from a diabetic coma that he didn't know he was suffering from. In fact, nobody from his family or friends was aware of it, even I did not know that he was going through such a disease that would cost him his life. And his sudden demise influenced Andy deeply, and he couldn't cope with his loss.

When Fred lost his battle of life, it was a very hard time for Andy. He was very shocked and quite upset, too. He couldn't believe that he had lost such a great mentor and a dear friend. That entire night, he stayed in his room, all alone by himself, recalling the old memories and remembering Fred with precious memories. Then he started praying to God to forgive himself for all the wrong thoughts and feelings he had and for all the wrong actions he committed.

When anyone believes that they are a sinner, and all of us are, then we need to make those choices for ourselves. Do we continue on our path and make our own way, or do we decide to follow Jesus and accept him as our savior? He took our sins on himself as he was crucified, buried, and then, three days later, rose from the grave.

Several verses talk about the significance of asking for forgiveness for your sins to lead a beautiful life in this world and the one after this.

Romans 3:23 says, "For all have sinned and come short of the glory of God."

In Romans 5:8, it explains: *"But God commendeth his love towards us in that, while we were yet sinners, Christ died for us."*

Romans 6:23 also explains about the afterlife. *"For the wages of sin is death; but the gift of God is eternal life through Jesus Christ our Lord."*

Romans 10:9-10 is about salvation, *"That if thou shalt confess with thy mouth the Lord Jesus, and shalt believe in thine heart that God hath raised him from the dead, thou shalt be saved. For* *with the heart man believe unto righteousness; and with the mouth confession is made unto salvation."*

Romans 10:13 says, *"For whosoever shall call upon the name of the Lord shall be saved."*

Those verses from Romans, the New Testament of the Holy Bible, are very common to anyone, especially the people who are in full-time service and work in a church. It's very fondly called "The Romans Road."

Then, verses that speak about a man being called into ministry are:

Matthew 6:33, *"But seek ye first the kingdom of God, and his righteousness; and all these things shall be added unto you."*

Mark 16:15, *"Go ye into all the world, and preach the gospel to every creature."*

1 Corinthians 7:17, *"But as God hath distributed to every man, as the Lord hath called everyone, so let him walk, and so ordained in all churches."*

***

Being a pastor and continuing this journey to walk on the path provided by God and religion is not easy. It is filled with difficulties and challenges because it isn't like a 9-5 job. Instead, it has no time limits. Your assistance and help could be required anywhere, anytime, and you have to provide your helpful services to any member of Christianity.

A pastor isn't an ordinary person. Instead, he is a very special and honorable member of the church. Just by the name that has a great religious meaning, you can tell the importance of that title. This great individual holds the authority to lead religious services. Pastors used their knowledge and insight to help lead others regarding the church services and in worship as well. In simple words, he is the main leader of the church, and nothing can happen without his notice or attention. He has been ordained to conduct all the religious services, including marriages, funerals, baptisms, and any other religious issues that fellow Christians face.

Being crowned as a Pastor seems easy, but it has a lot of responsibilities attained to that title. Before being seated in that great position, you must have a deep love for God and Jesus, and you should be ready to give it all for your religion. That person must desire to spread the message of God on earth and allow others to grow closer in a relationship with God.

No matter how severe the circumstances may be, he must continue doing the best he can for every member of the church. Whatever need, illness, or problem the church members might be having, a pastor must show his full support to these people. His calling in his job is to serve the members of the church in whatever they require assistance. Be it just listening, counseling, or giving biblical guidelines from the verses in the Bible. He should always be there for them and offer prayer. Once he becomes a Pastor, there are several verses that are really helpful for members of the church in several ways.

To encourage the members of the church:

- Philippians 4
- John 14

- Isaiah 40

To give hope and strength:

- Isaiah 40:31

To comfort:

- Deuteronomy 31:6

For strength:

- Psalm 46:1
- Isaiah 40:29
- Ephesians 6:10

For difficult times:

- Isaiah 41:10

Most meaningful:

- Proverbs 3:5-6

One of the most famous:

John 3:16

There are many other verses as well that are used by pastors to help people heal and stop them from hurting. There are certain ones as well that are aligned with the purpose of uplifting and encouraging them to pray with more focus and devotion. Hence, a pastor must have a great understanding of all these things about their relationship with God, and he should know how to help people in different situations.

That's why a pastor is like God's representative on Earth, helping people and guiding them. He is a person with many different roles, and he always looks up to God for further wisdom, guidance, comfort, emotions, sacrifices, peace, love, leadership, and relationships. It is how he develops himself into becoming a great role model to all the people and goes beyond his way to help them.

As the saying goes, "All things to all people." This clearly means doing things that will please others and being there for them in the specified way that they desire – just like a Pastor.

Andy was also taught about all these things, and he went onto this path after aligning his soul, mind, and body with his relationship with God. It gave him a purpose: to sustain a living that God and Jesus explained, and as he followed that trail, it led him toward a great journey. Andy finally became a pastor and poured every ounce of his efforts into doing everything for God, his religion, and fellow human beings.

However, the entire journey that led to this great victory in the form of pastorship wasn't easy. Andy had to go through a lot of obstacles to reach there, but his efforts paid off in the end. Taking it back to the time when I was still in the youth department, and Andy was in the Air Force, we didn't have the slightest of ideas that he would go onto this trail of greatness.

I still couldn't forget the time when that news broke to him. Andy and I were sitting together, and we were playing and singing the last song after the pastor preached. Andy was squeezing my hand but was not going forward to pray with Brother Thorpe. Now, with just the chorus remaining, Andy finally stepped out. Brother Thorpe was waiting for him because they had had a word earlier.

After the songs were over and they were done with the prayers, Andy smiled and seemed extremely happy. Gently, with a cute smirk, he returned to where I was with Brother Thorpe, and they both stood before me. Then Brother Thrope asked me what I thought about him surrendering to be a pastor and going to Bible College for some good training.

I jumped with joy and said I was thrilled because that was the only thing I wanted for him my whole life. He was really keen on serving God full-time, and now, since he had a chance to do it, I definitely wanted him to go there and become a pastor.

Brother Thorpe was also very happy and prayed for both of us and our life together, serving God. It was undoubtedly the greatest day of both of our lives, and I was glad Andy was fortunate enough to live his dream.

***

Now, it had been several months since Andy had been holding this big responsibility. During that entire phase, every situation he faced led him to a belief that whatever God wanted him to do, he was all he strived to accomplish. It became his life's purpose.

Then, with everything he did, it was always to the best of his ability to serve God. He worked on his sermons, sometimes for weeks, about merely a little thought he had on a verse or for a statement that he read somewhere.

Andy had a small notebook. He always kept it in his shirt's pocket with a pen. So, whenever he had something on his mind, be it a thought, confusion regarding something, or an explication of verses, at times, he also wrote down the verses or poems that sparked his attention. Later, in his office at church or at home, he would study more about those listed things and gain more relevant knowledge regarding them. That's how he always had a great sermon to preach.

It wasn't an easy thing to do all these sermons and win the hearts of the church members every time. Andy spent several nights preparing these. Sometimes, addressing issues would be so challenging that he had to spend some weeks finalizing the points. Although God helped him a lot in this process and inserted new ideas in his mind, he was able to deliver a great sermon.

Andy was also very wise about the Bible and invested his proper time and energy into learning the actual meaning of the verses. In this process of learning and enhancing his knowledge, he prayed to God for his constant guidance and wisdom. With his endless efforts and enthusiasm, every place he pastored applauded him for his exemplary services.

The last church he pastored in was around a small town in Texas, and it had a population of about 1600 people. Most of the people lived within the town's city limits, but during the summer, the population rose to about 10,000 people around the lake.

Andy was chosen to be the pastor of one of the churches in that town, and he started his service with just 24 people, and the number count increased to 191 people on his 11th anniversary as a pastor.

Everyone respected Andy because he was very kind and generous and didn't hesitate to jump in to help others. Besides working at the church, he also worked with the local fire department as the department's chief. The fire department where he volunteered and offered his services was pretty close to our house as well. Furthermore, he also worked with the pastor groups in the area, and in 2005, he went to Baton Rouge, LA, after the awful hurricane. It was very destructive, and Andy stayed in Baton Rouge for two weeks, and then he went to New Orleans and stayed there for four weeks.

***

Andy was serving God because it was what God wanted him to do. He wanted to see Andy help others and be the greater man. He even kept asking God to pour more compassion into his heart so he could serve the Almighty more. Then, it started to become clear how everything had a bigger meaning to it, and we all did what was expected of us.

Later, Andy and I both started serving God together with the help and alliance of one another. Andy was the pastor, and I worked as the pastor's wife, who was to minister to the ladies in the church, teach kids, watch babies in the nursery, sing specials, and do anything else that needed my assistance.

Slowly, things started getting more in sync, and we were able to live up to God's purpose more profoundly. Andy was doing a great job as a pastor, and with me on the side, working as the pastor's wife to teach kids – we both made a great team.

With time, I started reading more Bibles every day and started looking for more things that could align my purpose of existence with God's. I wanted to find out what more He wanted from me so I could work in that trajectory and make Him happy with my deeds.

Andy and my relationship grew stronger after the pastorship. We both were doing everything that was expected of us, and it turned out to be great. We prayed more, began reading the Bible together, and even studied some good Christian authors. These little yet meaningful things that we did together as a couple made me draw more toward Christianity, and I liked the great change it was bringing to me. In fact, it was easy for me to do all of it with Andy because I trusted him.

I would admit that there were many times when I depended more on Andy than God, but over the years, with constant reading and detailed studying of the Bible, things slowly started to change. Then, I could finally see my purpose and the reason why I was sent here, doing what I did.

I certainly have gotten closer to God in these past couple of weeks because I strive every day to study and pray for God's leadership, guidance, and wisdom to help me get through any situation that I face. It enabled me to find my true potential, get into this unchartered territory, and land on possibilities God expected me to accomplish.

***

Our church building could only accommodate 150-175 people, but for Andy's funeral, a tent was set up outside the church lawn for more than 50 – 75 people. It was around 2010, and everything was set up properly and systematically. There was a proper sound system, and every room had different speakers, including several sets of chairs to accommodate the guests.

Andy's death was even headlined in the newspaper, with a full-page write-up for him. Around 250-300 people came to see him one last time, and the church was flooded with people. Two helicopters were used for care flights, and they were faster than an ambulance. The Police Bag Pipe player from Dallas was there to play "Amazing Grace."

There wasn't a huge distance from the church to the grave. So, it was easy to take Andy's body to the graveyard. Moreover, there were at least 100 vehicles, which included fire trucks from all the Fire Departments within the county. It had two cars from the Texas Rangers Police Dept, the Local Sheriff's Police Dept, etc.

Andy was loved immensely by everyone in and out of town. That's why all these honorary people were at the funeral as well. It included a huge list of pastors, local pastors, and friends and missionaries from Mexico, Lebanon, Hawaii, and Japan. All these people especially visited the States to attend Andy's funeral. Even my daughter's boss came from Connecticut, and my son's pastor came from Houston, Texas.

If I recall correctly, there were five people who spoke about him. There were three pastors, a missionary from Mexico, and the last one was from the Fire Department. The main pastor who shared some good and wise words of remembrance for Andy was the senior pastor we worked with in Massachusetts for 15 years. Andy was his assistant Pastor.

Chapter 9: Surgeries

Most of my life had been compromised due to several health conditions. I wouldn't even be exaggerating if I said I had borne a lot of difficulties because of it. And the worst part was that my condition would trigger anytime and anywhere. Whenever that would happen, we would have to rush to the hospital, and then the endless procedure of pain and discomfort would leave me in shambles.

My health had always been something that I battled with since I was 12 years old, and it got more triggered after the death of my father. All that stress over the years contributed to my health condition, which kept worsening with time. Eventually, it took me to the hospital bed when my stomach pain got way more severe instead of getting better. At that time, I was crying in pain – it was that bad.

After undergoing several tests, the doctors diagnosed me with endometriosis. Back in the day, I had no idea what it was or what it meant, so they had to explain it to me in detail. I was told that this was a condition that apparently attacks the ovaries and causes immense damage. The doctors further explained that stress is mainly the underlying cause of it, and it often intensifies the pain.

I had to go through a major surgery when I was just 14. The doctors removed cysts from both of my ovaries, while the main focus was on the right side because it was affected more by it. Unfortunately, the situation didn't get any better, and it was just a temporary relief.

Then, I had to go through another operation at the age of 16. This time, while treating the cysts, they also removed my appendix. It was undoubtedly the most painful and awful-period in my life., I think it was an unlucky June because my beloved grandmother, Mama Tops, passed away around the same time. Her death deeply affected me and left me more engulfed in stress.

It was a cruel summer, and my husband, Andy, was working at a church in Kansas. I had a lot of plans and was really excited about it, but then we had to cut our stay short and return home in August because the doctors in Kansas said that I needed another surgery immediately.

This time, when I was hospitalized, it was the most difficult time of my life. They had to remove my right-side ovaries, fallopian tubes, and part of the uterine wall. It was an unbearable pain, but the operation helped. However, this surgery was physically wrecking, but it all caused wreckage on both of us (Me and Andy) mentally too. I was told that with this surgery, my chances of getting pregnant would be less. It was so devastating because Andy and I both desperately wanted to start a family.

For recovery purposes, I was advised against traveling from Texas to Missouri. Hence, I had to stay back and couldn't join Andy when he started his second year of college. So, here we were, only a year into our marriage, with Andy in Missouri and me in Texas – a great way to celebrate our union of love.

I was finally able to meet Andy at Thanksgiving when he managed to come home. It felt great to have him around, but little did I know that it was just the beginning of something turbulent. I had no idea that my health condition was going to decline pretty terribly over the next few years. All of those incidents took a toll on me, but I fought through all of them fiercely. Now, let's go back and recall those incidents in detail.

***

After my father's death, when I was 12 years old, my health started to deteriorate. I found myself getting crushed by many health issues, which seemed to be inherited from my family. My father had battled heart disease, and unfortunately, I got it from him. Along with that, the stomach issues were passed on from my grandmother. In addition to facing stomach problems for some time, she was later diagnosed with stomach cancer. This heartbreaking illness took her from her family, leaving behind nine children, with seven of them still at home.

Back in those days, she couldn't get diagnosed properly, and her condition remained a mystery to doctors. However, some said that it seemed like a severe case of endometriosis, which mercilessly attacked all her reproductive organs. Now, I was walking down the same path of fate as hers, and it was nothing but extremely painful.

As months passed, the pain kept doubling up. There were times when the pain stayed for months instead of weeks. And I couldn't even describe what those sleepless nights seemed like. It was like living your worst nightmare, and there was no escape from it.

Being just 12 years old and still recovering from the recent loss of my father, I couldn't help but get lost in the darkness of fear. I was scared to go through surgeries and witness all those painful procedures again and again. The doctors prescribed medication to help me manage and alleviate my anxiety symptoms. Some of those medicines were to make me sleep – I was barely sleeping during those days.

I was taking medicines, one after another, unbeknownst to what they did or what they were for. There wouldn't pass a day when I would skip any of these medications. I was doing everything suggested by the doctors and took every medicine on time, but still, my young mind couldn't help but imagine the worst. I was dreading, thinking of all the negative things like how I would meet the same end as my father. The death ringers were alarming around my mind, leaving me petrified.

I was completely asleep when they took me to the hospital for an operation. In fact, I don't have any memory of anything that happened during the operation until I got back to consciousness. I was given such a high dosage of medication that left me feeling nauseous as I woke up.

All these medicines were for my own good, but I felt they made me sicker. They made me throw up everything for six continuous hours. It was agonizing to a greater extent, but the nurses were very helpful and kind.

The combination of post-surgery pain and never-ending sickness only aggravated the uneasiness. Fortunately, amidst the ordeal, I found solace in my mother and Joyce, my mother's best friend, who had acted as a pillar of strength for me over the past five years. Joyce was there with me all this time, treating me with tenderness and offering comfort. She even helped me grow out of my fears a little bit, and I was glad to have her around. All the time she was there, she held my hand and kept rubbing my back – telling me it was going to be okay soon. The care and affection she poured into me during that phase surpassed even the care provided by my own mother. In fact, it wouldn't be a lie if I said she was a better mother to me than my own mom.

I was really exhausted after the surgery, and after a while, I slept as Joyce was caressing my back. When I woke up, I felt so much better. It was living, having a rebirth with a renewed sense of relief. My mother was still there by my side, and she told me about the doctor's report. She said, "According to him, the endometriosis had spread throughout my body, and he did a scraping procedure to remove it from unaffected areas."

I remained in the hospital for a few days. The doctor also informed my mother that there might be some damage to my left ovary and that he would monitor my pain in the coming months to determine the progression of the condition.

I experienced either no pain or mild discomfort for a couple of years following the surgery. It was really relieving to unlock myself from the cages of devastation. However, when I turned 16, I found myself back in the operating room, this time undergoing an appendectomy alongside further treatment for endometriosis.

***

Even after all the treatment for endometriosis, I couldn't get better. The pain was always there and couldn't completely go away. However, the severity of discomfort got slightly better during the birth of my first daughter. Even during pregnancy, the pain miraculously subsided, and it made me really hopeful. I was thinking that maybe I would get rid of this issue soon.

After my daughter was born, the pain returned, and it was worse than before. I kept struggling to lead a normal life, but I failed. It made me feel so powerless, and I felt that pain was coming in between me and my daughter as I would not be able to give her the attention she deserved. And it wasn't like that there was a fixed time or anything. I would normally be sitting, putting my daughter to sleep. Then suddenly, I would get this dreadful feeling as if every bone was crushing inside my body – the pain was that bad.

Within nine months of my daughter's birth, I got pregnant again. This time, it was a son. However, to my fortune, the pain disappeared during pregnancy one more time. For that entire duration, while I was carrying him in my womb, I didn't feel any pain, and it felt great to be able to live free without those ugly cries that come with that suffering.

I felt as if that pain was waiting for the birth of my son, and it returned with a vengeance after that. It was during this disturbing period that my doctor informed me that the pain would only worsen over time.

Given the severity of the pain and the diagnosis, I didn't have any other option but to proceed with a complete hysterectomy. It was a procedure that involved the removal of my uterus and other reproductive organs. The doctors were positive about it and spawned a seed of hope, saying that it would eliminate all the sources of pain. I finally thought I could go back to living a normal life once again.

The doctor discovered how extensively my internal organs were damaged during this surgery. In fact, he said that a hysterectomy should have been considered earlier, looking at the severity of my condition.

However, I couldn't help but thank God, who helped me conceive my two children before undergoing the procedure. And the miraculous thing was I had them despite being told I couldn't have kids. It filled my heart with joy and made me grow closer to God. All because of him, I was able to bring two precious lives into the world despite the challenges I faced. It made me have more faith in the kindred spirit and build an association with HIM.

In the end, the partial hysterectomy took away my right ovary and fallopian tube, but it also provided a glimmer of hope for a better future without pain and devastation. It was an exhausting journey, filled with moments of despair and uncertainty. Yet, I held onto the belief that a higher power had guided me through the pain, allowing me to experience the joy of motherhood despite the trials I endured.

***

Talking about it again takes me back to the golden old days of school. Throughout my school years, participating in basketball and softball provided me with a great opportunity to get away from the house and indulge in these healthy interests. Since I belonged to a sports family and everyone was a bit too inclined toward sports, engaging in these activities was more like a natural choice, and my family never questioned my involvement.

However, a few years after my children were born, I started experiencing persistent pain in my right wrist. It was then that I first learned about carpal tunnel syndrome from a friend's mother, who had just gone through wrist surgery recently.

Curiosity always kills the cat, and in the same way, it took me to my doctor. Out of inquisitiveness, I decided to consult my doctor regarding the pain in my wrist. After conducting some tests, he confirmed that I needed carpal tunnel surgery. It was around 1985, and the procedure was rather complicated. I vividly remember the excruciating nerve block in my arm, which marked the most painful experience I had ever witnessed.

Following the surgery, my hand and arm were covered in bandages, and the doctor said that it would require around six weeks to heal. Six weeks, and that too with an immobilized hand wrapped in big bandages, was not easy, but I think it was worth it as it brought me relief. Thankfully, the surgery turned out to be beneficial, and that discomfort from my right wrist was gone for good.

For six years, everything was going great. I didn't feel any pain, nor was there any kind of discomfort. However, right after that, the pain in my right hand resurfaced. My thumb seemed to have developed a condition known as trigger finger, where it was bent and stuck in the same place. In fact, my thumb had gotten so stiff that I had to use the force of other fingers to straighten it. It was extremely painful, and I couldn't do anything with that hand and had to rely on the other hand even for the smallest of tasks. I was getting quite frustrated by it. My functionality was getting affected, and slowly, it started to take a toll on me. So, I had to go through another surgery to counter that pain.

Four years after my initial carpal tunnel surgery on my right hand, I had to undergo the same procedure on my left hand. The doctor explained that most cases of carpal tunnel surgery occur after an injury or due to wrist fractures in the past. In my case, I had broken my right wrist twice during my school years — once in grade school and again in junior high. Furthermore, after marrying Andy, we continued our sports involvement and played in a church softball league. During one of the games, while I was fulfilling my duties as a catcher, I got a fracture in my left wrist when an opposing team member slid into my home. Then I got another surgery for it.

***

Almost 11 years ago, I found myself wrestling with excruciating pain in my Achilles muscle, the area at the back of my ankle. The doctor informed me that this injury had occurred during the years when I used to play softball as a catcher. Squatting for an extensive period of time to train myself to become a great catcher had worked against me. Slowly and gradually, it took a toll on my Achilles, and it reached a point where I couldn't even walk properly without support.

To address the issue, I underwent another surgery. It was not that complicated, but it did hurt really bad. About eight weeks after the surgery, I was on a knee scooter, and during that phase, six of my friends were helping me to get around my apartment.

Subsequently, I transitioned to wearing a walking boot for an additional four weeks. Finally, for four more weeks, I wore a regular walking boot without any cushioning inside. Gradually, I regained the ability to walk almost normally without any discomfort.

However, my journey with surgeries did not end there. Several years later, I had to undergo a full knee replacement on my left knee. The surgery happened in the morning, and then in the evening, medical professionals got me up and made me walk a short distance down the hall.

I went to the same care facility where my mother was admitted. It was for a four-week duration, but I started showing massive progress within two weeks. My commitment to daily exercises allowed me to complete my rehabilitation in approximately two weeks.

***

It felt as if there was no stop button to my suffering. Every time when I thought it all would be over, another health-related problem would come knocking on my door. This time, it was the breast cancer that turned my life upside down.

I used to get my mammogram every year, which is a special test for evaluating breasts for any unusual changes. During one of the tests, the results came out quite shocking. Looking at the reports, the doctors asked me to come back in three months for another test.

When I underwent the other test, and it showed the same concerning results, the doctors suggested doing a biopsy. It is like a test when they take a small piece of tissue to inspect it more closely.

I was quite confused, with no idea about what to do. So, I went to a special doctor who treated patients with breast cancer and other conditions like that. He immediately did the biopsy and found out that there were spots on my left breast. Since it was a serious condition and required immediate action, he scheduled breast surgery three days later.

Even though only one breast was affected, my children suggested having a double mastectomy. They thought it would be better to be safe and not have to worry about more surgeries in the future. Then, I also consulted with the doctor, and he advised me the same thing. So, we decided to go ahead with a double mastectomy.

The surgeon put something called breast expanders in my chest to make room for implants that would be put in later, after a few months. But right after the surgery, one of the expanders got infected and had to be taken out. Then, within three days, the other expander got infected, too, and I had to go back into surgery to get it fixed.

The next day, I had an emergency surgery to remove one of the implants. My plastic surgeon performed it, and right after that, I was scheduled for another surgery after three days to get it completely cured.

Some people from my church were present during the last surgery as well. One of my friends called our pastor, and he prayed for me throughout the entire duration when I was in the operation theatre. My daughter-in-law was also there.

The next morning, my plastic surgeon told me that he only could remove the implant and wasn't able to clean everything properly. He further explained that once I healed from the infections, he would do one more surgery to clean everything up.

After the double mastectomy, I had to have two to four drains for about two months. It was a very painful process and always caused an uncomfortable effect. This process went on for about seven months in total. The first surgery was in October 2018, and the last clean-up surgery was in April 2019. It felt like a never-ending time, and then I felt the clock had gone slower.

Not following the calendar, but just remembering the many years of surgeries. In 1980, I started having trouble eating. No matter what I ate, my stomach would hurt a lot, and I would feel sick. It was really worse when I ate greasy or spicy food. So I tried to avoid those things, but when it got out of control, and the pain was unbearable, I had to consult a doctor about it.

When I went to the doctor for this issue, he ran some tests and, after examining me, said I needed to remove my gallbladder. He suggested going through surgery next week before the situation gets more critical.

It took a couple of weeks, but after the surgery, my situation got better. Then, I was able to eat anything without getting sick. I still had to be careful about what I ate. Once I started following a proper eating routine, things got much better pretty quickly. I didn't have to struggle with that condition for too long, luckily.

***

All my life, I never had any problems with my teeth until I started feeling a strong pain whenever I chew on something hard. I always brushed my teeth twice every day. I thought it would help with the pain, but it didn't. And when the pain didn't go away, instead, it kept worsening. Even reached a point where my face and head also started hurting a lot. That's when I realized I needed to go to the dentist or the oral surgeon.

The oral surgeon did some X-rays and, after a thorough examination, said that my wisdom teeth were doing the damage. He said it would be best if he removed all four of my wisdom teeth at once. I had no idea how it all worked and what I should and shouldn't do, so I agreed with whatever the doctor told me.

They put some numbing thing over my teeth, and they put me to sleep. When I woke up, all four of my wisdom teeth were gone. I did have some pain afterward, but thankfully, it didn't last very long. It wasn't anything unusual, and I would always be grateful that it was one of the few operations where I didn't experience a hefty amount of pain. Although it was still enough to make me uncomfortable, it was less severe than the other surgeries I had gone through.

Undoubtedly, my life has been a roller coaster ride, and sometimes, I survived without a belt on. My health condition tried to pull me down in every way it could, but I was persistent and wanted to change my destiny. So, I kept fighting, pushed hard, and thrived for better days. Finally, I was able to get through everything and got better.

Chapter 10: Rhode Island

When I met Andy, I felt a sense of complete relief. Andy was my rock, providing me with the support and stability I needed to get through the tough times. We were each other's life partners, and I knew we could overcome anything life threw our way together.

Andy and I went through our share of ups and downs, as any couple would. But marriage has been my greatest achievement, one that I am proud of. It gave me strength, security, and the courage to keep moving forward.

Soon after my surgery to have my right-side ovary and fallopian tube removed, during my second and third years of college, tragedy struck as I experienced the heartbreaking loss of a baby. The following years were marked by anguish and suffering, and I lost hope of ever becoming a mother.

However, fate had a surprise in store for us. I received unexpected news that I was pregnant during a routine checkup at my OBGYN's office. Overwhelmed with joy, I immediately sought out Andy, who was working at a church. As we embraced, tears of happiness streamed down our faces. We felt immense gratitude for the divine blessing bestowed upon us.

My pregnancy, though, was far from easy. Throughout the entire gestation period, I battled intense sickness, not just in the morning but throughout the day. In order to support Andy's career as an assistant pastor, we decided to move to Massachusetts. By the time I reached the seventh month of pregnancy, our anticipation had grown as our baby was due on

September 17th. However, the sickness persisted, extending beyond seven months and continuing until our daughter's birth on October 12th, 1974. It was an unusually long pregnancy, lasting almost ten months. Despite the challenges, our happiness knew no bounds when we finally held our beautiful daughter in our arms. We felt immensely blessed. With time, our family grew, and we welcomed our son, Craig.

As a family, we cherished annual vacation trips, alternating between Texas and Massachusetts, depending on our place of residence. One particular year, when Cheryl was about two years old and Craig was just a few months old, we embarked on a road trip and then back to Texas. We ingeniously modified the back of a Pinto Station Wagon, creating a play area for Cheryl and a small travel bed for Craig. Seat belts were not as strictly enforced in 1976, so one of us would drive while the other tended to the needs of our children.

As the kids grew older, our road trips became more interactive. They would bring along activities to keep themselves entertained, and we engaged in various games during the long drives. One of our favorite games involved finding objects starting with each letter of the alphabetical order or guessing an object based on descriptive words. These simple yet entertaining activities brought us closer as a family, fostering laughter and togetherness.

However, a memorable incident occurred during one of our trips through Pennsylvania. The kids repeatedly spotted signs that read, "Watch out for falling rocks." Curious, Cheryl inquired whether it meant that rocks would fall off the hills or mountains and onto the road. Just as I was about to answer affirmatively,

Andy chuckled and concocted a whimsical story. He shared that it was the name of a young Indian boy who had lost his way while hunting, prompting his father to put up signs seeking help from passersby to locate him. According to Andy, people had been searching for the boy for years.

Innocently believing the story, Craig responded with sadness, exclaiming how unfortunate it was. From that point on, whenever we encountered these signs during subsequent trips, our children would feel a twinge of sorrow. It took them over five years to realize their father had invented the story. Initially upset, we eventually shared a hearty laugh, and it is a lighthearted memory that still brings us joy whenever we spot a "Watch out for falling rocks" sign.

After serving as Assistant Pastor under Reverend Armstrong in Massachusetts for almost a decade, Andy received an exciting opportunity. Reverend Armstrong informed him that the older pastor in Rhode Island was retiring and asked if he would like to try out for the position. Andy eagerly accepted, and Reverend Armstrong contacted the retiring pastor to arrange for Andy to preach at the church.

However, Andy faced some unexpected obstacles. I had just undergone a complete hysterectomy, and we were hit by a massive snowstorm, declaring a State of Emergency and restricting access to only service vehicles. As a result, Andy was unable to attend the first week. Nonetheless, he finally arrived the second week of February 1978.

Despite the challenges, Andy ended up being offered the role of pastor. However, he needed to be ordained first. Four pastors from the area formed Andy's council and extensively questioned him about his beliefs and knowledge of the scripture. I was also asked to share my experience of inviting Jesus into my heart. Thankfully, we both passed and celebrated with a party in the Rhode Island church. The gathering included sandwiches, chips, drinks, and a cake shaped like a cross made by a lady from the Massachusetts church. Several members from both churches and many of Andy's family members attended, making for a joyful and unforgettable night.

***

Moving to Rhode Island turned out to be one of the happiest instances of our lives. We were hesitant at first as we were unsure how it would pan out. But eventually, we took the plunge, and it turned out to be one of the best decisions we ever made.

The joy and blessings that we received through this decision were immense. We found a sense of purpose and fulfillment in our lives, and our kids also thrived in this environment. They were able to experience the beauty of a close-knit community where people were always there to support and uplift one another. They could participate in various youth groups and activities that helped nurture their faith and spirituality.

Andy also found renewed fervor in his work and his faith as he was able to serve in a capacity that he truly believed in. He led and guided our community with love, compassion, and wisdom. The church also provided us with stability and security, allowing us to focus on other important aspects of our lives.

When we first moved into the church basement, we weren't quite sure what to expect. But from the moment we arrived, we felt welcomed and at home. Our kids were delighted - they loved exploring every nook and cranny of the church and quickly made friends with the other children who attended.

One couple, in particular, stands out in my mind. Their kids were the same age as ours, and they hit it off immediately. We were relieved and thrilled that they had so readily found playmates. The mother of that family quickly became a dear friend of mine. Whenever I had to help with church activities, she would give up her time to babysit my kids, who adored her and her children.

It wasn't just the kids who found friends, though. Andy and I both made great connections at the church. I loved getting together with some of the other ladies to go shopping or grab lunch, and Andy enjoyed catching baseball games with some of the guys from the church. They often went and watched the Pawtucket Red Sox play when it was baseball season. They were a Triple-A affiliate of the Boston Red Sox.

Overall, our five years at that church were beautiful. We felt like we had become part of a community and had found a place where we belonged. It's an experience we'll always cherish.

***

The cozy apartment in the church's basement was a hidden gem, featuring two bedrooms, a bathroom, a kitchen, and a comfortable living room. Separated from the three other church classrooms and a women's restroom, the living quarters offered a private escape for the pastor's family.

We were greeted with a warm and inviting atmosphere upon entering the apartment. The living room was spacious and attractive, with a designated area for a dining table and chairs, ideal for family meals. However, due to the big table and chairs already in the kitchen, we transformed the dining area into Craig's bedroom instead. The room had a comfortable bed, a dresser, and a toy box, rendering it perfect for Craig.

Cheryl had one bedroom, and Andy and I had the other bedroom. The back stairs, located conveniently by the kitchen, led up to the church's upstairs and the outside parking lot where we kept our car.

The apartment featured a large 10-burner gas stove in the kitchen, making meal prep for our family of four a delightful experience. The converted living quarters were a true testament to the men of the church's hard work and dedication to our family's comfort and well-being.

Once every month, I would have a gathering of women at my apartment. During this time, we would read religious texts and briefly discuss them. Afterward, I would ask people to share their prayer requests, and we would pray together to conclude the meeting. I generally prepared coffee and a tasty treat, and we enjoyed ourselves.

Craig's birthday happened three weeks after moving into the apartment. Some women discovered it was Craig's birthday, so they gave him a small scooter that he sat on and moved by pushing it with his feet. He enjoyed riding it all around the apartment. Then, Andy would come and open our door. Craig then rode it back and forth in the hallway outside our apartment. Then, he and Cheryl would alternate turns to ride it. It was a fun sight for me.

Craig was four years old, and Cheryl was five years old at that time. Cheryl went to kindergarten at a school nearby, and Craig and I would walk her there in the morning. Then, in the afternoon, we went back to meet her and walked back home together. At first, Craig felt sad when she went to school. But later, he diverted his attention by riding his little scooter everywhere in the apartment, pretending to be in a race and consistently winning.

Our apartment living room had a metal pole on one side. Our furniture was arranged to place the TV on the wall opposite the pole. The pole was in a good spot for the kids to lean on while they watched cartoons on TV. Often, Cheryl would rest her body against the pole while Craig lay down with his head on her lap. She would gently rub his back. It always touched my heart to see them like that. They loved each other a lot and always got along well.

When Cheryl was at school, it was evident that Craig missed her endlessly as he would stand by the pole and watch cartoons alone. Craig got up one day while I was making cupcakes. He looked away from the TV slightly and accidentally bumped his head into the pole. There was a large bump on his head. He received a cupcake after he stopped crying, and I held him until he stopped. After that, he returned and sat down, resting his back against the pole. After a short while, Andy returned home.

Craig got up, ensuring he didn't hit his head again, and went to his dad to say hello. Andy noticed a bump on his head and wanted to know how it happened. Craig grabbed his hand and brought him back to the living room. He sat down briefly but then stood up and accidentally bumped his head on the pole. This caused another bump to form on his head. Of course, I was worried, but I have to admit it was a bit funny how he demonstrated what had happened to his father.

It was almost time to pick Cheryl, so Andy suggested they would all go and get her. She felt sad when she saw the bumps on his head, but Andy advised her not to inquire about what had occurred to Craig, or he might injure his head again. We all enjoyed the story and laughed about it a lot.

A church helper named Mr. Swanson came every Saturday to clean the auditorium and tidy up the church hymnals. He used to clean the carpet by running the vacuum cleaner back and forth in the aisles. Andy had an office next to the auditorium. Sometimes, while Andy was studying in his office, Craig would play with him in the office.

One particular Saturday, Mr. Swanson started using the vacuum cleaner. Craig left the office and went to unplug it from the wall. He was not as tall as the top of the pew, so Mr. Swanson could not have seen him. Craig would hide underneath a bench while Mr. Swanson would reconnect it and begin vacuuming again. But then Craig would just disconnect it and hide again. Mr. Swanson was getting angry because he didn't know what was happening. Craig unplugged the cord twice more before Mr. Swanson caught him.

Mr. Swanson brought Craig to the office and informed Andy about Craig's actions. Andy laughed but told Mr. Swanson to tell Craig that he would punish him and ensure he didn't unplug the vacuum again. Craig and Andy went back into the auditorium. Andy warned Craig not to unplug the cord again, especially if Mr.

Swanson was vacuuming. "Yes sir," Craig said, and he never did it again. The following week, Mr. Swanson was using a vacuum cleaner. Craig came out of the office, walked over to Mr. Swanson, greeted him with a "good morning," and extended his hand for a handshake.

Mr. Swanson liked that and showed Craig how to straighten the hymnals. Craig then went around the auditorium and fixed every hymnal book while Mr. Swanson completed the task of vacuuming. Mr. Swanson was impressed with Craig's work and rewarded him with $3. Craig was pleased. He spent the following weeks fixing the hymnals, and every week, he earned $3. He was delighted about making money, so he stopped causing problems for Mr. Swanson, who, in turn, was happy that Craig was doing a good job.

Mr. Swanson started liking Craig and even invited us to dinner at his place. We all went, and Mrs. Swanson immediately took a liking to Cheryl as she helped set the table. They both loved our children, and our children loved them too. We all got along well. Sometimes, the Swansons would watch over both children on certain Friday nights, allowing Andy and me to have some time alone. They didn't have any children, but they loved ours a lot. They always spent more money on presents during Christmas than we did, or sometimes almost as much. Their gifts always came from Santa. We were fortunate to have the support of nearly everyone in the church.

In the face of physical struggles and the heartache of loss, our journey to parenthood was marked by resilience and unwavering hope. The challenges we encountered strengthened our bond as a couple and as a family. We found the courage to press on through sickness and laughter, cherishing the precious moments and embarking on memorable adventures together. As we continued this chapter of our lives, we carried with us profound gratitude for the blessings we received and the joy that our daughter and son brought into our lives. Little did we know that more incredible chapters awaited us in our family's story pages.

Chapter 11: Texas

Looking back, I sometimes wonder if I made the right decision and if I should have faced my inner battles and the chaos for the sake of paying my respects to the woman who had given me life. But life is often filled with choices that don't have clear answers and decisions we have to live with, whether they bring us peace or regret.

Cheryl and I stood at the cemetery on the bittersweet day, the anniversary of my mom's passing. The Texas sun shone down, making the gravestones feel both warm and sad. This place held not just my mom's memories but also the history of both our families, who had deep roots here.

Cheryl, being naturally curious, asked about other family members resting there. I showed her the graves of my aunts, grandmothers, uncles, and distant relatives. This cemetery was a place where generations of our family found their final rest, a reminder of the strong ties that bind us.

In the middle of the graves was a small chapel for quiet reflection. A plaque with our family name was a tribute to the many relatives laid to rest here, thanks to my mom's care for this sacred place.

***

In the summer of 1971, between my first and second year of Bible college, Andy and I found ourselves back in Boston, working hard to earn extra money for our education. However, what should have been a time of preparation and excitement turned into a heart-wrenching ordeal.

In June of that year, I began experiencing excruciating stomach pain. Seeking answers, I visited a doctor who conducted tests and then delivered devastating news. He told us that our baby had passed away and that surgery was necessary to remove the lifeless child from my womb. The weight of that news was soul-crushing, and the pain we felt was beyond words.

But, even in the depths of our grief, we clung to our faith and each other. We prayed for our lost child for over a year, hoping against hope that I would recover. It was during this trying time that we turned to the words of Genesis 50:20: "But as for you (the Devil), ye thought evil against me; but God meant it unto good." We believed that the Devil had aimed to hurt us, and indeed, he had succeeded in causing us unimaginable pain. Yet, through this hardship, God had a plan to draw us closer together and strengthen our love.

Becoming parents was a tough journey. After losing our first baby, doctors told us that my chances of getting pregnant again were slim due to endometriosis, which I had been dealing with since I was 11. I had already undergone three surgeries to fix things – one to remove a fallopian tube, another to remove my appendix and some surrounding tissues, and the third was a partial hysterectomy on one side. It seemed like the odds were stacked against us.

The pain I felt after going through a miscarriage was indescribable. It was a unique kind of grief that made me emotionally and physically vulnerable. Emotionally, I experienced a deep sense of loss, sadness, and even guilt. I mourned not only for the baby I lost but also for the dreams and hopes I had for that child.

Though I realized that it was natural to have feelings of emptiness, despair, and depression, coping with the idea that the pregnancy didn't progress as expected was just incredibly difficult. Physically, the aftermath of a miscarriage brought me immense physical discomfort and pain. But the grief was greater, as society does not always acknowledge it in the same way it does other forms of loss. Every life has a measure of sorrow, and sometimes, this is what awakens us because it made me grateful for what I already had.

For three long years, we tried to have a baby without success. But then, something incredible happened. We returned to the town and church where Andy and I first met. He was working as an assistant pastor there. Against all odds, I became pregnant. It was like a miracle, reminding us that sometimes, even when doctors say it's impossible, faith and hope can make the impossible happen.

The whole period of my pregnancy was relatively normal manner, even though "normal" for me meant being sick all day for five months. But I guess it was just a way for me to understand that after painful days, God blesses you with a beautiful gift in the face of a baby. Just waiting for my blessing to come, I endured the pain as bravely as I could. No doubt that my husband was a great support and was by my side, giving me the relief I was looking for.

Andy's work at the Texas church lasted for a year before we boarded on a new chapter, moving to Massachusetts. There, he assumed the role of assistant pastor under Reverend Armstrong, a position he held for nearly two decades. Our lives were taking shape as we built a family together.

In October, after a full nine months and a few extra days of anticipation, I gave birth to our daughter, Cheryl. The joy of becoming parents was overwhelming, and we were on cloud nine with our precious baby girl. Andy's parents lived above us during the first few months, and their sustenance made those early days even more special. They practically became regulars in our apartment, sharing in our happiness.

Eventually, we moved to a better apartment in Brockton, and Andy's parents began their journey to live with his older sister. Yet, they remained a cherished part of our lives, visiting our new place at least once a week.

When Cheryl was almost seven months old, she and I went on a journey to Texas to visit my mom. We spent a memorable 2.5 weeks there, creating precious memories. Our lives were filled with love, and we couldn't have asked for more.

Nine months later, God again blessed me, and we welcomed our son, Craig, into the world. This pregnancy and birth were perfectly normal, and Craig arrived just one day before his due date, the best day of our entire lives. I couldn't even express my feelings at that time; I was so overwhelmed.

That was the moment in my life that made me see that our journey takes us through tough times, setbacks, and unforgettable sorrows. But in the end, it cherishes us with blessings when we least expect it. Finally, the joy of becoming parents was a reminder that hope and determination can lead to miracles, even when things seem impossible.

Andy and I tried our best to raise our children with all the love and care that they deserved. Whether it was granting all their wishes or giving them the guidance to make them good adults, we did everything in our power. Andy always cooperated with my parenting style, as he always had my back. My children were my miracle; I just wished to give them the best life possible.

As our children were growing up, I remember we used to take those road trips where we went to see our family members. Every year, whether we were living in Massachusetts or Texas, we would hit the road and make the trek across states. These journeys were more than just travel; they were family adventures filled with laughter and memorable moments.

Our usual route took us through Pennsylvania, and it was during one of these drives the kids noticed the signs along the side roads that read, "Watch for Fallen Rock." Cheryl, ever curious, asked what it meant, and that's when Andy, with his boundless imagination, spun a story for them.

He told them about Fallen Rock, the name of an Indian boy who had lost his way and was still wandering, trying to find his way home. He encouraged them to keep a close watch, suggesting they might see him along the way. Their little faces filled with wonder, and they watched the passing landscape with rapt attention, giving Andy and me a precious break as we held hands and continued driving through Pennsylvania in peaceful silence.

For the rest of the day, our kids whispered to each other, imagining where Fallen Rock might be sleeping at night, what he was eating, and how he spent his days. They even asked if we would come back the same way on our journey home, eager to look for Fallen Rock once more. Andy assured them that we would.

On subsequent trips, the children continued their quest to spot Fallen Rock along the side roads, and each time they did, it became a cherished family tradition. Even after we returned home, we would all share a good laugh whenever we saw those signs, remembering the imaginative tale and the joy of family adventures.

I can never forget the lightheartedness and family bonding, reminding us that the simple moments and shared stories create lasting memories. It's proof of the power of imagination and the joy of spending quality time together on the road of life.

Chapter 12: Breast Cancer and COVID

Just like all individuals have different personalities, both my kids were also very different from each other, with a few similarities between them because, after all, they shared the same blood. My daughter Cheryl was very outgoing and extraverted like her dad, who could talk to anyone easily, even if she was meeting them for the first time.

In the later years of his life, he would go to the mall and sit to talk to anyone who passed by or sat next to him. However, I did not like shopping because of the chaos at the malls, so I preferred to stay back whenever he went on unless I really needed to shop. Cheryl adopted the same nature as her father, and she had always been friendly and approachable with quite a lot of friends in her social circle.

Craig, on the other hand, was nothing like her because he took after my personality. He would remain silent and observe people until he got to know someone better. He would never trust people easily and would not talk much till the time he felt comfortable around them. He only had one or two close friends. Craig was someone who would rather stay inside and play with his toys, whereas Cheryl would always go outside and play with her friends.

Cheryl always wanted to hang out with her playmates, and they remained the same throughout their grade school and junior high years. Even though both of them had good friends at the church, Craig still preferred to stay home and play. Throughout their grade school years and junior high, I kept getting sick very often. I used to have really terrible migraines that would cause me to actually pass out, and I would be admitted to the hospital for 2-3 days, not knowing anything about it.

We had a terrific friend who took care of the kids in my absence, but Cheryl, being the elder sister, would often take care of Craig. She would stay close to him, and if other kids tried to pick on him, she would take care of them, and the two siblings would go play by themselves. If lunch was fixed for them, she would get Craig's food first and then her own. Even when Craig was a baby, and she was about 2 or 2.5 years old, she would get me his diaper and wipes so I could change it, and then she threw the diaper away because I was in a lot of pain from the endometriosis before surgery for a complete hysterectomy. She helped me a lot even though she, herself, was a kid.

As I got better and was able to work, everything got better. Cheryl was back to herself and started dating, being busy most of the time. The more she stayed away from home, the stronger and more independent Craig became. When he got into high school and started in the choir and drama club, it was then that he slipped into his own aura. We began to witness some notable changes in his personality as he became much more outgoing and made several friends. He was an excellent singer and led the worship music team in his church.

He participated in dramas in high school, which also gave him confidence because he was quite skilled at it. He even won the best actor award in his senior year and sang many specials at school and church. Cheryl and Craig were undoubtedly the best adults I could ever meet, and no one could be prouder of them than me because I was their mother. I have never known such talented young men and women as my children, and I am not saying this because they were my kids, but even other people used to complement the same. Both of them have always had excellent jobs in places of responsibility and worked for their employers consistently, which was a testament to their work history and commitment.

Craig has had a long, happy, and lovely marriage for almost 30 years to my loving, excellent daughter-in-law Shelly, who was actually more like a daughter to me. They gave me the most beautiful gift in the form of my two grandkids. Since I am their grandmother, I do not see any flaws in them, and they seem perfect to me, at least. Corey, my grandson, is married to Rachel, who is a terrific wife, daughter, sister, daughter-in-law, and great-granddaughter-in-law. She is also a wonderful mother to Della, my great-granddaughter, who is beautiful, talented, smart, and already the best 2-year-old in the history of the world.

Craig's other child is a beautiful girl named Caitlyn. She is a gorgeous young woman who cares for everyone and is a great singer as well, just like her dad. Both Corey and Caitlyn are different from each other, as their father and his sister were. Corey is more like his father, and Caitlyn is more outgoing like her mother and Aunt Cheryl. I have also inherited another granddaughter, Kara, who was born from Joe's previous marriage. She is married to Jermaine, and they call me Nanny. Just like my other children and grandchildren do. I love them all more than I can ever express. These are my family members, and there is no other mother ever who could be prouder and happier to have each of them in my life. They have given me countless hours of happiness, and I am absolutely content and thrilled that they continue to bring me happiness by taking care of me in my old age. I feel so blessed that I am surrounded by such caring people when I need them the most.

I have lived a happy life, and even during my youthful days, I had people to look after me. I had a caring husband, a loving mother, and beautiful kids. I remember that after working in the church in Central Falls, Rhode Island, for almost five years, Andy felt that he should go back to the church in Massachusetts for only a short time as Reverend Armstrong told us he was moving back to Texas and asked Andy if he wanted to pastor the church in MA. Andy refused, and within two weeks of us leaving Rhode Island, the church in Texas called Andy to come back and be the assistant pastor for a second time.

The current pastor was going through some physical problems, and they needed a faithful pastor to take control and take care of everything like a senior pastor would. So, Andy and I moved back to Texas with our kids. Cheryl and Craig graduated from Canton High School in MA and started working in downtown Boston. Cheryl took up a job at a travel agency, and Craig worked as a shoe store manager until he and Shelly moved to Houston, Texas. Shelly belonged to Texas, and that is where the two chose to get married.

Andy and I moved back to Texas in 1997 at the same church again, where we met until 1999, when Andy was called to Whitney, Texas, and we stayed there until 2010 when he passed. Cheryl stayed in MA with one of Andy's sisters until she moved to Connecticut and started working for an Aerospace Co. where she still works today. She has a wonderful relationship with the man of her dreams, Joe, who loves her greatly and is a terrific son-in-law to me as well. He is certainly an asset to our family. Joe also has a fantastic family that has welcomed us as part of their family. Cheryl has become a loving mother to Kara, and she is also a wonderful stepdaughter to Cheryl.

While Andy was in the Air Force, he was stationed at the Shepherd Air Force Base in Wichita Falls, Texas, where my mother and I lived. Andy's roommate was the son of a preacher in St. Louis, Missouri. Jim said one Sunday morning that he was going to church, and Andy said, "I'll come with you." They walked into my church that morning and continued to attend church there until Andy was finished with his four years. After he got out of the Air Force, we got married and went to Bible College.

During those four years, he had become really good friends with the pastor and preached a few times. After Andy finished college, the pastor asked the deacons and the church to take a vote for Andy to come back as an assistant pastor after graduation. We stayed there for one year, then moved to MA in 1974, and Andy started working for Reverend Armstrong. He was a fantastic preacher and taught Andy almost everything that he had learned as a pastor. We love the Armstrong family very much.

***

There were a lot of times when I was in the hospital for 2-5 days because of passing out from the pain of migraine. The migraine used to be so intense that I would pass out somewhere in our house, be it our bedroom, our bathroom, our living room, and almost anywhere. This happened for about 10-15 years in a row, but I am glad that now it is very seldom that I get a headache. I vividly remember that I was in Texas one time, visiting my son, daughter-in-law, grandkids, and great-granddaughter, when I started feeling under the weather one day. I did not pay much heed to it as I thought it was nothing serious and that I would be fine; however, it continued into the night as well.

When I felt that it could be something grave, I finally called my granddaughter in the next room, and she got my son and daughter-in-law. Shelly got the blood pressure machine, and I measured it to check that it was high, with my heart rate at 42. We watched it for a couple of hours, and when the situation did not improve, I decided I needed to go to the ER. They kept me under observation for a while, and the pressure in my chest started getting worse, with my blood pressure getting critical as well. They transported me to the hospital since the ER was a different building from the hospital. They were operating separately. At the hospital, they watched me for a couple of hours with my BP going higher, the heart rate dropping even lower, and continued heart pressure.

Then they called the Cardio Doctor in, and he performed a heart catheter on me to check for a blockage, but there wasn't one. They admitted me and kept me under observation for the rest of the night and the next day as well, and then let me go home the following day. They also mentioned that if I lived there, they would put a pacemaker in. Since I had to leave for home in a few days, they did not do anything but give me a letter from the airport informing them about the essentials that I would need on the flight. I made it home safely and then visited my personal cardiologist, who I had been seeing, and everything was OK.

In 1997, Andy and I had recently moved back to Texas, and he was working for the church that we met in. We both worked, with Andy at the church and me at the Red Cross. I started feeling sick again but thought it might just be the flu. It just kept getting worse until Andy called my mother to ask if she could take me to my doctor because he was in a meeting. My mom drove over and took me to my doctor. They immediately took me back and ran an EKG, and since it did not look good, they called for an ambulance. The ambulance came and took me to the ER, where they did an EKG along with a blood enzyme level test, which would show if it was a heart attack or not. They watched me for a couple of hours, which gave Andy enough time to get there, and then the doctor came in and broke the news to us that I had had a heart attack. They had taken me to the catheter lab, performed a catheterization on me, and unblocked two of my arteries with angioplasty.

After having my angioplasty done, I started having a lot of cardio issues, and about every 4 or 5 months, I used to be back in the hospital. The doctors would then do another catheterization where they would put a stent in or do an angioplasty again. Within less than two years, they did catheterizations five times, put in two stents, and also did my angioplasty three times. In the meantime, Andy was called to Whitney as a pastor, so we had to move. I started going to a doctor there, who then referred me to a cardiologist in Waco.

My new cardiologist in Waco said the first problem I had was with the treatment I was getting. He said he would put me in the hospital and do more than just minor repairs like they did before. Nearly six months after moving to Whitney, I had heart problems and was sent to Waco to be checked into the hospital. They did a catheterization the next day just to see what needed to be done and how bad my condition was. Then, two days later, they did my quadruple open heart bypass, and I was in the Cardiac Critical Unit for three days. However, I recovered well enough and spent another five days in the hospital.

My son and his family were there, and the hospital had three rooms for family where they stayed for three days. After that, Andy was to stay in my room with me on a fold-away cot for another eight days, and then my son and his family went home. When I was discharged from the hospital and went home, my son and his family came back for the weekend so they could spend time with me and take care of me. My daughter also flew down and stayed for two weeks to help take care of me. I was doing much better when Cheryl went back to Connecticut.

It certainly took me months to feel almost back to normal. I clearly remember that after six weeks, I went back to the hospital for physical therapy, and that went on for an additional twelve weeks. By then, I was feeling much better and kept getting stronger by the day. I was beginning to feel much better, with no heart pain, which was a great sign.

After a little while, the COVID pandemic kicked in, and we were to follow strict quarantine. And when that was over, we were still required to wear masks and stay six feet apart from other people. The Sr. Pastor at the church I was going to was really sick as he had lung cancer, and the assistant pastor was taking over. He said that we did not have to wear a mask while we were in church. However, I kept wearing my mask because I had a very low immune system since I went through breast cancer and took chemo treatments and infusion treatments.

Soon afterward, the Sr. Pastor passed away, and the assistant pastor prepared the funeral. The funeral was to be held the next day, and he was doing all the arrangements in front of me. I noticed that nobody was taking any precautions related to COVID, as no rule of being six feet apart or wearing a mask was being followed. And just within three days of the funeral, I fell sick, so to be on the safe side, I went to a drive-through clinic for COVID testing. And to my horror, the test results came positive. My doctor then prescribed me medications for it, but within another two days, it became extremely difficult for me to breathe.

A friend then took me to the ER, and they took me in and put me on the COVID floor of the hospital. They ran tests on me and discovered that I was not only COVID-positive but also had double pneumonia. I was admitted to the hospital right after the news broke, and I was there for five weeks constantly, being given breathing treatments and different medicines for COVID. They did not exactly know what worked, so they kept changing my medicines from time to time. I was not allowed to have any visitors, and it was really difficult being alone and so sick at the same time. But as time passed, I gradually got better.

During that time, my daughter called and said she thought it would be better if I moved to Connecticut so she could help take care of me. Since I had no family in town, within a month after being discharged from the hospital, my daughter arrived to help me move. We packed my belongings and relocated. To be very honest, I love it in Connecticut and did not miss Texas at all, maybe because my daughter takes such good care of me, and my mind is always occupied with them. Nonetheless, I feel blessed to be surrounded by such a loving and caring family.

Chapter 13: Whitney

Firstborns are extra special for parents. Similarly, Andy, too, had a distinct place in his parents' hearts. Throughout my life, I have always tried to do something special for his birthday because when he was born, he got really sick and was in the hospital for a couple of months. The doctors were not hopeful that he would survive and had called his parents to the hospital several times and told them that he probably wouldn't live through the night, but luckily, he did. His mom absolutely loved narrating that story to everyone so much that as he got older, he would even ask her about the time he was in the hospital. He would ask this question in front of the entire family, even though none of his siblings wanted to hear the same story again and again.

However, Andy always thought that it was funny, and then his mother would tell this long story about how they had initially gone to the doctor for one of his older sisters. But when the doctor saw Andy, he stopped examining and said he needed treatment as he was sick. The doctor asked Andy's mom to take off Andy's clothes, and then they sent him to the emergency room. His mother was left crying, thinking she would never see him alive again. But, again, he survived, and that is the reason why I always went all out celebrating his birthdays.

I vividly remember this one time, to celebrate Andy's birthday, when our children, Cheryl and Craig, sent letters out to everyone in the church and Andy's family back in Massachusetts in Rhode Island. We had them stay in Texas so Andy wouldn't know about the surprise. After everyone had arrived, I told Andy that we had to go to the church and pick up something. When we walked into the church, most of the church people were there, along with our children and grandchildren. One of his brothers had come with his family, and both of his older sisters were also present. As soon as we entered the church, Andy was shocked to see his family. It was just so thrilling to see his face and how excited he was because we had worked on a bunch of different posters that included Andy's pictures through the years. It was like a trip down memory lane for him.

We had everyone gathered around the fellowship hall at the church, and then one of the deacons got up and announced that they were really excited to share Andy's 60th birthday. He further explained how everyone was so thrilled about the surprise and also informed Andy that all the deacons had voted on giving him a three-week vacation per year that he could take whenever he wanted. Most of Andy's family stayed for several days, and we had a great time together. I remember we went to a rodeo one night, and they absolutely loved it. After spending a few days with us, everyone flew back to where they had come from. Our kids stayed for a few more days, and then, after everyone had left and Andy and I were sitting in the living room, he broke down in tears.

He said that it was the best and most memorable birthday of his life. When our kids invited everyone, they had mentioned that instead of getting Andy gifts, they should give him money so Andy and I could go on vacations together. Andy always wanted to go to Florida to watch the baseball games of spring training in March, so we began researching how we could do it. I made a few phone calls, ordered some tickets to a couple of the Red Sox spring training games, and made reservations at a hotel for a week and a half. I even bought a dog carrier to carry our little Chihuahua Pomeranian with us. We drove to Florida, and on our way, we stopped at one of the churches that we knew about in Florida. Andy preached at that church, and they gave him a love offering, so we had even more money on our hands.

After that, we drove down to the hotel, and we stayed there for several days. We had our fair share of adventures as we drove down around Florida, enjoying little things. I remember we went out on an airboat ride with the dog one day and saw alligators for the first time. We also drove out close to NASA, where we found this little church near Vera Beach, and we went to that church on Wednesday night. They were having prayer time when we stopped there, so we just joined in, and they wanted us to come back on Sunday. When we went back, Andy preached there, so they gave us a love offering. We went back on Wednesday night and had a great time. I remember the pastor said,

"We'd love for you to come back on Sunday and preach again if you're still going to be here."

Andy said, "You know, we were planning on going home, but there are still some games that we would like to see, so we will be here Sunday morning."

So, instead of going home after a week and a half, we stayed for another week and a half, and we saw 13 baseball games. We watched the Cincinnati Reds, the Los Angeles Dodgers, the New York Mets, the St. Louis Cardinals and Boston Red Sox play. We went to different stadiums, and we actually came home with a little bit more money than we had gone down there with. It was because Andy preached several times at that church on our drive back home. After coming back, he said that it was absolutely the best vacation that he'd ever had, even better than the one when we rented the RV and took the kids to Niagara. He loved it and of course, so did I as we got to spend every minute of three weeks with each other so it was the best time of our lives. In less than two years after that, he was diagnosed with esophageal cancer, and on May 5th, 2010, Andy passed away. We had our vacation in March 2008, and the Lord knew I was going to lose him, so he gave me those three weeks to enjoy life to the fullest with him. It was undoubtedly the best time of my life.

But I guess every single day that I spent with him was the best because we had a remarkable 40-year marriage. Being in the ministry for 38 years, having two beautiful kids, four beautiful grandkids, and a fantastic daughter-in-law, what more could we ask for? Every day of our marriage was even better than the previous one. I have never regretted marrying Andy Andersen, and I guess it was the best decision of my life. That vacation to Florida was one of the best times of our marriage together. He was completely thrilled that the Church had done as much as they did, but they always gave him a love offering for his birthday and for our anniversary. He said it was the best gift that God ever gave me.

I remember that I was given this little dog by one of the church members who had been abused. She was part Chihuahua and part Pomeranian and a beautiful little dog. She was very smart and got disciplined in only one attempt as she was a fast learner. I recall having a hard time naming her, and that is when Andy finally came up with the idea that both of our kids' names started with C, and both of our grandkids' names also started with C's, so we decided to call her 'CC' from that day onwards. She was an absolute sweetheart; however, she didn't care too much for Andy at first. Maybe it was a man who had mishandled her previously, and that is why she did not like men. We took her out for a walk every night, and after coming in, Andy used to give her a dog bone as a snack so she could get familiar with him. He did that until she became more familiar with him, and then she would go out with him to do her business and then come back and sit down with him. She would look up at him until he gave her a snack, and she learned that really quickly. She would still spend more time with me and sit with me every night as we watched TV, and she did that for several years.

Then, at the end of 2009, she started sitting with Andy occasionally, at least two or three times a week. She would jump up in his lap if we were sitting in the living room watching TV. For some reason, he had started to become tired, so he would come home for lunch, rest a little, and then return to the church. He had a bunch of different things that he liked to do for the church, and that's what kept him busy. I remember when the kids got together at Christmas time in 2009, he was very tired and wasn't himself that Christmas. He would go to bed early, which he usually did, but this was earlier than normal, or he didn't have the same appetite that he had before since I was busy with Christmas preparations at that time, so I did not say anything. I did not even notice all of it except that CC was sitting with him more and more.

I can never forget that it was January 13, 2010, and Andy had an upper G.I. and a lower G.I. appointment on the same day, at the same time. The VA often did preventative appointments and stuff to keep their servicemen healthy, and on his doctor's appointment that day, I was sitting in the waiting area waiting for him to come. At that time, the doctor came out and called me to accompany him into another room so he could talk to me. I went after him, and he said that in Andy's procedure, they had found some polyps in his colon that he was certain were cancerous. But he cut them all out, and he thought that everything was going to be fine. However, there seemed to be a problem with his adrenal gland, but the worst thing was he had seen a lot of Barrett's Esophagus, which was cancer. He could not remove all of it, and he did not even try because it was so extensive that he said he would have to schedule surgery for another time but that Andy did have cancer.

So, I went in with Andy and waited for him to wake up. And I told him what the doctor had found, and he said surely that couldn't be true because he was not finished yet. I said I know, but it is true, and we're going to meet with the doctor in a couple of weeks, so I drove home that day and called our children. I told them what was going on, and our son said,

"Mom, I'll be there with you that day," I replied, "Thank you." I needed that moral support as it was a very difficult time for me. Andy told the deacons at church, and one of them offered to be with him if Andy was fine with it. Another deacon said that it must be why CC had been spending more time with Andy; she probably sensed that there was something wrong with him. You know, animals sense those things much faster than humans can ever do. So, we went back to see the doctor in a couple of weeks, along with our son Craig and one of the deacons who accompanied us during our visit.

After a thorough examination, the doctor said that the whole esophagus was pretty much all cancer and the only thing that he could figure would be the best treatment was to do surgery to remove the esophagus. He also explained that he would have to bring the top of the stomach up to Andy's throat and reattach it there, and he would be on a feeding tube for a while until everything healed. He said that after a while, they would remove the feeding tube when Andy would recover. Andy asked him if he would lose his voice, and the doctor replied that he did not think so. Andy told the doctor that no matter how dangerous the surgery was, he wanted to go through it because he wanted to keep preaching to the world. He also said that he did not want to lose his voice, so the doctor said they would do the surgery at the end of April.

He went back to the hospital within the next few months and had some different treatments, which included a PET scan and an MRI. His surgery was scheduled for the mid of April. On the day of his complex surgery, there were 27 people at the hospital for him. Some of them were church members, a few family members, and some other pastors had known Andy for years. It was a 17-hour surgery that he underwent. It was very painful waiting all day, and then he was in recovery for hours. We couldn't even see him until the next day, and when we did, he had tubes going all over the place. Of course, he couldn't speak, so I bought a small write-on wipe-off board for us to communicate. That way, I would ask him questions, and then he would write his answer on the board and vice versa. I am extremely grateful to my sister and her husband as they pulled their fifth-wheel RV down to the hospital. There was a small RV park next to the hospital and a building that had showers and baths inside, and we could also receive mail or send mail through the office part of that building as well. The RV that my kids and I were staying in was nice as it had a sofa-style bed that my son would sleep on while my daughter and I slept on the queen-sized bed in the back of the RV. We also had our own shower and bathroom, and we also had a kitchen.

Every day, there were four hours when we could not go to Andy's room because of the HIPAA laws that required nurses to change shifts. So, it was two hours in the morning (6:30-8:30 am) and two hours in the afternoon (4:30-6:30 pm). We would utilize that time to have our meals, and we did this for three weeks. My son had already been out for three weeks, so he had to go back two weeks after the surgery. However, my daughter was still with us when Andy was moved to a single room, and we could stay with him as much as we wanted to. However, he got C diff, and my daughter caught it as well, so I had to take her to the doctor, and she could not be with him. When she got better, she flew home after Andy came home from the hospital. He had not even been home for 24 hours when he fell sick again, and Cheryl had flown back by that time. I had to rush him back to the hospital, and he was so sick that they actually put him into a coma so they could control some of the sickness instead of him continually throwing up and ripping the incision. Since it was attached to the throat, it was very sensitive, and the doctors had to ensure nothing happened to it.

I clearly remember that it was May 5th, and my daughter-in-law was with me at the hospital while my son and daughter were still at their home. They were working, but Andy started getting in bad shape around 9:30 or 10 a.m., and they would not let me go into the room. Finally, around noon, they let me go in, and I promised that I would just go over to the corner and stand. The doctors had been in there working on him with the nurses, so when I walked into the room, I said, "Andy, I'm here with you." He had a lot of tubes going everywhere, so he couldn't talk, but he heard me because he smiled and then closed his eyes forever and went on his journey to meet the Lord. I took my kids on a conference call and informed them that their father had passed away.

Shelly's mom drove my son and two grandkids up to our house that evening, and a little bit later, Cheryl flew in. Shelly, my daughter-in-law, went to the airport and picked her up, and Andy's siblings also flew in the next day. A good friend of mine worked at a bed-and-breakfast there in the town. We did not have any hotels or motels, but she arranged for Andy's brothers and sisters and everyone else who flew in to stay there at the bed-and-breakfast. My mom came to our house and stayed with us.

Chapter 14: Funeral

It was May 5, 2010, when Andy passed away, and his funeral was held on May 10. Andy's funeral was a very emotional affair for not just his family but also for all those people whom he had an impact on during his life. The town that we lived in was based on a small community, and ours was one of the probably five or six churches that we had there. Andy had been at that church for about 12 years as a pastor until he had to go through a long procedure for the removal of his cancer; he passed away a couple of weeks after his surgery.

The church's auditorium could only hold 150 people, but we had around 300 at Andy's funeral. Hence, the reason for setting up an additional sound system for the Sunday School rooms downstairs and outside is that we had to set up a tent.

One of the speakers who spoke at Andy's funeral was a missionary from Mexico who initially grew up in our town, Whitney, but later moved out. He was back and forth in our town, sometimes a couple of times a year, and he was one of the five different speakers at Andy's funeral. Several of the other pastors in the Dallas-Fort Worth area who taught and worked at the Arlington Baptist Bible College had all come in. Some missionaries came off the field from Mexico; one of them was from Hawaii, and one came back from the Philippines. We had different singing groups in the church at one time or another, and they were all there.

All of my family and Andy's entire immediate family were present there. Even Cheryl's boss flew in from Connecticut to attend Andy's funeral. My son's pastor and many of his church members in Houston came up. A lot of firemen who belonged to the county and had come with their fire engines were present at the funeral. The volunteer fire department within the county itself had arranged 15-20 different vehicles, fire engines, and other kinds of fire equipment trucks. There were local police, sheriffs, and the Texas Rangers police force.

Five ministers spoke at Andy's funeral. 2 of the ministers were from the Arlington Baptist College, one of which was the President. It was heartwarming to see that so many people that Andy had worked with had come for his funeral, including a fireman and the pastor who had been with Andy in Massachusetts and worked together for 20 years. This pastor preached the funeral service.

The firemen spoke highly of Andy's leadership and how caring and considerate he was toward every call they made. He narrated how Andy always wanted to comfort people whose belongings had been destroyed by the fire and calm them down to release stress. He spoke of Andy's dedication to never saying no to anyone who ever asked him to preach a sermon anywhere.

The fireman explained how Andy would always volunteer for anything. Whenever he wanted Andy to be at, whether at the college, to preach or carry out chapel services, he would always agree to it. He never let down anybody or returned them empty-handed when they came to him with any request.

Listening to the fireman, one of the other pastors also got up and delivered a small speech. He told me how Andy always gave 110% to everything. He elaborated on how Andy worked for more than 40 hours a week when, normally, everyone else would only put in 40 hours most of the time. At that point, what surprised me was the fact that even after working so much, Andy still managed to make time for me and his family and never compromised on his relationships. He even visited regular people and the members of the church who were admitted to the hospital. If somebody was having an important surgery or any kind of procedure, he would go to their home and would pray with them. He would calm them down and would try to help them work things out. He would always be available on call and did whatever other church members needed. It was a unanimously established fact that Andy was a very helpful soul who always put other people's needs before his own.

The main speaker at Andy's funeral was the pastor Andy worked with for many years. He and his wife were both there, and he proudly spoke of the determination to do whatever needed to be done in the church. Then, with his permission, he read an article from the newspaper about Andy's death and from Andy's journal. Ever since he found out that he had cancer, he began to write about his family in a journal, particularly about each of his children.

He had mentioned how he was so proud of our daughter Cheryl for paving her way into a successful career in Connecticut all by herself. He was gratified that she had made good friends and settled well in a new place. Andy also wrote that he was proud of our son, Craig, who was using his talents to sing and lead the music in his church. He was also always content about how great Craig was as a father and how well he was keeping up with the tradition of the other Andersen men who were great fathers.

Andy was glad that Craig had learned from his dad and grandfather and never let him down. He had also mentioned Shelly, our daughter-in-law, and how she was such a great wife and a perfect mother to our grandchildren, Corey & Caitlyn. He mentioned that they were a great family, and they served in church and always participated actively in all the church activities.

He had also written about our grandson, Corey, and how proud he was of the young man that he had become and how he was still going to become a lot like his father and even his grandparents. He had mentioned how Corey had the will and strength to do things he loved and utilize his talents. He was quite friendly, extroverted, and an excellent example for young boys his age. Everyone who met him absolutely adored and loved him. According to Andy, Corey will become an even better individual when he grows up, and he cannot wait to see his accomplishments, but sadly, life does not give him a chance.

He also mentioned Caitlyn ~~Kaitly~~, our granddaughter, and said that she was an extremely cute little girl who was lively and funny. He told her that nothing was impossible as the word spelled out, "I'm possible," and he wanted to give her confidence that she could do whatever she wanted. He told her that God loved them and would support her in all her endeavors.

Finally, Andy spoke about me and elaborated on how he loved me more than anything else in the world. He wrote a very emotional note that if he did not survive the surgery and went to heaven, he would ask God to replace my guardian angel because he wanted to become mine so that he could stay closer to me and take care of me. I knew one thing for sure: Andy would always put in effort without me knowing, and his love and concern for me were always beyond belief. Andy was undeniably the best soul I have come across in my entire life, and I can't wait to reunite with him in heaven one day!

The funeral took about two hours, and after that, the fire department that Andy was associated with pulled up their main truck to the church's front door. They carried the casket out, and a bunch of firemen got together, raised his casket, and put it on top of the main engine going to the cemetery. The procession consisted of firemen from each one of the eight volunteer fire companies, and each one of them brought their own engines. The county even took out two of the helicopters from service, especially for Andy's funeral, and they hovered over the church during the entire service.

There were numerous official vehicles that were part of the procession headed to the cemetery, and then there was one family car, and the rest of the people drove in their personal vehicles. The drive from the church to the cemetery was about 7 to 8 minutes. There were a few pallbearers, including two of Andy's brothers, three of the Churchmen, and two guys from the fire department. Our grandson followed the casket when it left the church for the cemetery, and he carried Andy's Bible, which he had always used to preach from. I think he was somewhere between 12 and 15 years old and still did a great job for a boy his age.

The police department's bagpipe player from Dallas came up and played Amazing Grace. The fire department that Andy was connected with had placed his empty boots at the end of the coffin and his helmet on top of the casket. They gave me his entire bunker gear suit, helmet, and boots. Nobody else ever wore those, as they were kept in Andy's memory. At the end of the funeral, one of the people in his fire department called out Andy's number and, for the last time, said, "1920 will never answer a call again because he's just passed away."

How great of a human being he was! I feel privileged to have had his companionship and to be called his wife. The 40 years that I spent with him were the best days of my life, and I will cherish every moment of it till my last breath! Andy was undoubtedly the most amazing man I have ever known in my life, and words can never do justice to what he meant to me.

Chapter 15: Texas Again

After Andy's death, I tried to do my best to ensure everything at his funeral went smoothly, and thankfully it did. Once I was finished tending to all the guests who had flown in from various places, I decided to stay in town for a while. At that point in time, I did not feel like moving out of our home-and starting a new life in an entirely different town or city. Thus, I stayed in there for a while until I was informed about my mother's deteriorating health condition. She had Alzheimer's, and her condition had slightly worsened at that time, partly because her husband was not taking good care of her. He had multiple issues going on with himself, so he had to be put in a nursing home, and as a result, my mother was left all by herself.

So, I decided to move back to my hometown to take good care of my mother and ensure she was doing well. After shifting back, I began to attend the church that Andy and I had first met in. Even though they had a new pastor at that time, many of my old friends were still there, so I did not hesitate to go there again. Initially, I did not intend to participate in any church activities as I intended to step back and be a normal church member. But then, one fine morning, I was asked by a lady to go to the altar and pray with her, so I did not refuse. After the service, the pastor called me into his office and told me that I could not do any altar work in his church as his wife handled everything. He clearly said that his wife would take care of the ladies who wanted to pray, or he would choose someone to do that. I was upset and told him that I had known most of these church members for about 30 years and had known some for longer than a year. I conveyed my message politely that I had no intentions of saying no to someone if they asked me to go to the altar with them and pray, and I would do it anytime they asked me to. I told him that I was not seeking it out, but if a situation like that presented itself, I would never say no to it. But he kept reiterating that I could not do it, and he did not allow me to do so, so I left that church.

There was another church in town, so I thought it would be OK to go somewhere else, so I went to this new church and met with the pastor. He was a really nice gentleman, and I really liked him as a person, so I started going to church regularly until COVID-19 hit the world. I also began to work part-time in town, and I became a school crossing guard.

After my second year, they made me the supervisor of all the crossing guards in town. It was an extremely big decision for me to move back to town and start returning to the church where Andy and I first met. But my heart was at peace, and it told me it was the right thing to do as everything was different now. Back in the old times, Andy and I used to go out with couples, but things have changed now, and I was not invited to go out with couples for obvious reasons.

Everyone over there used to be very cautious about things they said around me as they feared saying stuff that would make me miss Andy. I did not know who to talk to and who to avoid in a conversation because I always thought that if I told them how much I really missed Andy, they would become even more upset and worried about me. Hence, I kept it all inside me and never really showed my true sentiments in front of anyone. Then suddenly, COVID came, and literally, the entire world around us changed.

We went into quarantine for quite a long time, and right before the quarantine was over, I got double pneumonia along with COVID-19, and I was admitted to the hospital for about five weeks. I was not breathing well and was continuously struggling as I had headaches almost all the time, paired with a constant cough.

It was a very difficult time for me as I thought I would not be able to make it and my kids would also lose their mother after their father. However, God is gracious and merciful, and I survived. I was on three inhalers after getting discharged from the hospital, and I had a lot of medicines to take. Then, after a while, I began to get better; however, my breathing has not returned to normal as yet, although it has been quite a while now. I used to take breathing treatments after getting out of the hospital, and I had a nurse who used to come and check me on a daily basis.

Most of the time, it would be the same nurse, and they would do physical therapy with me and make me do breathing exercises. They even brought a portable X-ray machine to my home to make sure that my lungs were doing fine. As I said, I have struggled a lot with breathing issues, and even to this day, some of the problems prevail, so it's been difficult living all by myself. After I was released from the hospital, my daughter called and told me that she needed me to come and live with her. She wanted to stay close to me to help and take care of me. Thus, doors began to close on me in Texas as fast as they were opening in Connecticut. My daughter went to an apartment complex and filled out an application, and I got my apartment within three weeks.

She came to Texas and helped me pack everything up; I sold a bunch of furniture, gave some of it away, and got rid of the bed because I could not sleep in it anymore. I clearly remember that one of the lovely Church members was very kind and gave me a twin-size hospital bed, which made it easier for me to breathe as it could be raised. Sometimes, I still find it difficult to sleep because when you have shared a bed with someone for 40 years, you miss them a bit too much at times. I used to miss Andy a lot, but I am glad I moved to Connecticut because I made some of the best friends that I have ever had in my life. The church that I still go to has a group of women who are very nice as they respect everyone and never bad mouth about any individual. They are genuinely pure-hearted people whose only purpose is to serve the Lord. I honestly don't know many of them, but I get amazing treatment from them and also from the pastor and assistant pastors, so I like my Connecticut church very much.

There were times when I found it hard to cope with my husband's death, but these ladies at the church helped me get through the tough times by lending me support without even having to ask for it. They are selfless people who never expect anything in return, and I consider myself fortunate to have found genuine friendships here in Connecticut. I love spending time with them, and finally, after four years, I do not have to think about who I need to hang out with. Happiness and sadness are part of life, but when you have good people around you, everything seems to be sorted. I go out with them for lunches and coffee, and I have also volunteered to be on the prayer time in this church. In Texas, I was told not to participate in church-related activities; however, nobody here stopped me from going up to the altar and praying, and that is what I loved the most!

This change has made a big difference in my spiritual life, and I love these ladies of the church for doing that for me; I respect them a lot, and I think that we have a great time together. We have small groups here where we are taught different subjects, and I enjoy it a lot as it has enabled me to be in the presence of some of the greatest teachers. I love my life here in Connecticut, and I do not have any complaints about my health because I think it's because I'm just getting older, so there's not much I can do about it.

Having to leave the church that Andy and I had served in for such a long time was indeed a tough decision, but I am glad I did it. I have come to realize that you serve wherever God wants you to serve. So, moving away from that church was what needed to be done because it wasn't where God wanted me to be. God wanted me to be in a place where I could get unconditional love and utmost respect and be acknowledged for being a pastor's wife. I have started to work a lot on myself, and now I study the Bible and listen to people delivering lectures about different subjects. When you interact with different people, you can get something out of everyone, and that adds to your knowledge. So, overall, I am incredibly grateful to the Lord for making me move to Connecticut and introducing me to this new life that I am really enjoying!

Chapter 16: Moving to Connecticut

When COVID-19 started, we went in quarantine for a while, and when it was lifted, I was all set to go back to work but could not. I was informed that they needed someone younger than me, and a supervisor wanted my job even though I had been at it for the past nine years. The management thought she could do it better than me because she was younger, so they hired her without telling me beforehand until I showed up for work on the first day after quarantine. I was a little upset, but then I applied for an unemployment fund and received it for a few months.

During this time, I was exposed to COVID. Since I had been through breast cancer already, my immune system was comparatively weak at that time. I was still taking a little bit of chemotherapy and some infusion treatments to build me back up after the chemo. It was my bad luck that I got COVID-19 and double pneumonia at the same time and was admitted to the hospital for five weeks. After being discharged, I realized that I needed to be close to my daughter so she could help me take care of myself. She flew down and helped me move in with her; we packed everything in a U-haul trailer and drove to Connecticut, where she lived.

I stayed with her and Joe at their house for about three weeks and enjoyed my time there. I kept some of the furniture I had brought with me from Texas, along with a bunch of my husband's books that he used to study alongside the Bible. They helped me greatly in numerous situations, and I am glad I took them to Connecticut. The month I lived with my daughter was great, as Cheryl and Joe made me feel really comfortable. Both of them were terrific cooks, so I was never hungry at all, and they made sure to make my stay at their house memorable. My daughter even took me to different doctors as I needed to take good care of myself. I had to find a new cardiologist, a primary care physician, and an oncologist, and I am grateful that I found great doctors here in Connecticut. The two of them took great care of me the whole time I stayed at their place, and then, after a few weeks, they helped me get an apartment in an elderly complex.

Within a month, right after Thanksgiving of 2020 and before Christmas, I moved into my place. It's been three years since I moved here and I like this place as there are only four apartments in each building and there are just seven buildings. I love my little one-bedroom apartment as it's quite a nice place, and everyone around gets along well. As stated in the previous chapter, I have made great friends and enjoy my company at the church because all those women are kind and genuine individuals. I also meet with a different group of ladies once a month, and during that night, we have a Bible study together. After that, we talked and laughed and had the best time together. The entire church team comprises terrific people who are always sweet to each other and care for everyone like their own family. They help others become better Christians by spreading positivity and love everywhere.

They care for people not just in the United States, but one group goes to Costa Rica every summer and works with a church over there. We send them money to help in their ministry and have an outreach in other places. It feels great to me to belong to an active church that cares about other people regardless of who they are or where they belong.

In our community, we try to do as much as possible by taking initiatives such as blood drives, collecting clothes and food for the needy, etc. I am enjoying this new life here in Connecticut so much that the only reason I would ever go back to Texas would be to see my son, who lives there with his family. I no longer desire to live in Texas, so I have decided to stay here in Connecticut as I love being close to my daughter. I am extremely happy and love my life because things have worked out well for me. God opened the doors for me very quickly and made me realize He is always there to help us get through all kinds of situations.

Cheryl, my daughter, and Joe are not married, but they share a happy life. Joe is a fantastic man who treats Cheryl wonderfully, and they make a perfect couple. Whether they decide to marry in the future or not, I'm completely fine with it. They have known each other for around 23 or 24 years, and seeing them together brings me immense joy. Their strong bond and support for each other make me happy as a parent.

Cheryl, who works for a company that involves a lot of overseas travel, finds comfort in her relationship with Joe. He's understanding and supportive and always gives her the freedom to pursue her job without worries. While Cheryl loves to travel, the separation from Joe has started to impact her, showcasing the depth of their love. It's heartwarming to witness their respect and affection for each other.

Joe also has a daughter, and the relationship between her, Cheryl, and myself is a source of happiness for all of us. The fact that Joe's daughter considers Cheryl as her mom adds to the family bond. I have also become a grandmother to Joe's daughter, which brings immense joy.

Being part of Joe's Italian family has been a delightful experience. His relatives, including his uncles, aunts, mother, and stepfather, live close by, fostering a sense of community among us. During holidays, I am expected to be part of their gatherings, and the acceptance and warmth I receive from Joe's family make me feel truly blessed. It's heartening to be embraced into this strong, close-knit Italian family.

One of the family members, Joe's great aunt, an incredible 102-year-old woman, is an absolute joy to interact with. Despite her age, she's so full of life, sweet, and deeply religious at the same time. Our conversations often revolve around our shared faith in Jesus. When we gather at Joe and Cheryl's house for dinners or special occasions, she insists I lead the prayer. Our mutual respect and beliefs contribute to the positive atmosphere within the family.

This shift from being part of a Texan family, where rodeos and barbecues were the norm, to joining an Italian family has been a wonderful experience. The Italian traditions, especially the delicious lasagna and other mouth-watering dishes, have added a new flavor to my life. The warmth and camaraderie shared during family gatherings create lasting memories, which makes me appreciate this newfound sense of belonging.

Being part of Joe's family has been a fulfilling journey for me. The love, acceptance, and shared traditions have enriched my life in ways I cannot comprehend. From the strong bond between Cheryl and Joe to the welcoming embrace of Joe's extended family, every aspect of this new chapter has been a source of joy and gratitude. I cherish the relationships formed and look forward to making many more happy moments with this incredible family.

Joe and Cheryl's connection began several years ago through a mutual friend, and as time passed, their bond deepened. Joe resided with his grandmother and formed a close-knit family with his daughter. Although I never had the chance to meet Joe's grandmother, I have heard wonderful things about her. She was widely loved, and everyone who knew her had only good things to say about her. Joe seems to have inherited her kindness and warmth and passes it on to everyone he meets.

Cheryl and Joe's friendship evolved into something more meaningful after both faced personal losses. Joe lost his grandmother, and Cheryl lost her father. That was when they found solace in each other's company, and their relationship blossomed into something special. Their compatibility is evident in their shared intelligence and culinary skills. Joe and Cheryl are known for hosting fantastic gatherings that always turn their home into a hub for family and friends during every holiday.

Despite being an "adopted" friend, I have seamlessly become part of their extended family. The atmosphere at Joe and Cheryl's house is filled with love, respect, and a sense of belonging. Whether Easter, Thanksgiving, Christmas or any other occasion, their home is the go-to place for all the joyous celebrations. It's heartening to witness the genuine happiness they bring to each other and those around them.

Cheryl and Joe's union is a blessing for themselves and everyone who knows them. Their happiness radiates and makes gatherings at their home a delight for all. I'm not the least bit concerned about Cheryl's well-being with Joe. His commitment to taking care of her is evident every single day, and I have full confidence that even when I'm no longer around, Joe will continue to ensure Cheryl's well-being with love and care.

Their journey from being friends to becoming life partners is a beautiful tale of finding solace and happiness in each other. Their shared experiences and genuine care for one another make their relationship special. As they continue to create cherished moments together, I'm grateful to witness the love they share and the joy they bring to everyone around them.

Chapter 17: My New Calling to My Lord

I am not a preacher, but I believe men are best suited for that role. I feel called to full-time Christian service and believe that being a pastor's wife, I can contribute significantly to his ministry. If a pastor's wife embraces a calling and actively engages in various aspects of church life, it can enhance her husband's work. I remember that during my time teaching teen girls, I enjoyed organizing a monthly Bible study and spending time with them every two weeks. When my children were small, I cherished serving in the nursery.

However, being a widow has shifted my interests, and now I desire a more focused ministry with other widows. My journey from active involvement in various church ministries to a more focused interest in supporting widows reflects a natural evolution driven by changes in life circumstances. Connecting with fellow women who understand the challenges we face is crucial for healing. I recognize the healing power of connection and communication among women facing similar struggles. My vision for this ministry includes regular gatherings, perhaps monthly, where widows can come together to share in prayer, games, or simple conversations. The fellowship gained from such interactions is vital for our healing process. To be a widow evokes special feelings, and it feels invaluable to be with other people who have gone through similar stuff.

I can say through experience that the pain of losing a beloved or spouse may never completely go away. Still, the empathy and support given by a group of women who have gone through the same situation may help us get through this challenging expedition. I am highly committed to the Prayer Team, and my prayer journal grows with new names and requests daily. The desire to serve others through prayer is a constant thread in my life. However, my current physical limitations have impacted my ability to serve actively in the church, as I require a cane or a walker at all times except when I am home. Despite these challenges, I believe in the importance of women actively participating in the church, especially if they are passionate about specific ministries.

I have built wonderful relationships and friendships with various ladies in my church. Some of us gather monthly for lunch, where we share all that happened with us throughout the four weeks, both the challenging times and our blessings. Our conversations are positive, and we focus on the goodness of God rather than gossiping about others, unlike some other women's groups who are habitual of these things. Our discussions cover many topics, such as our daily grocery shopping and the great bargains we find.

However, our primary focus is always spiritual. We explore the scripture together and decipher what it means in our lives. I can proudly say that the group of women I hang out with differs from other women's groups. We are a community of strong and spiritual Christian women connected to each other by our shared love and devotion for God, Jesus, and the Holy Spirit. Our utmost devotion to the Trinity is what makes our bond special.

Besides this, I am also part of a smaller group of about five women who meet once or twice a month. We gather at each other's places, go out for lunches, or simply gather to study the Bible, but whenever we meet, we always conclude with prayer. What makes our group special is our shared love for the Lord and our desire to serve Him. Our study of religious books differs; currently, we are working on the book of John, which has been a great study so far. We cherish our church and each other, and above all, we love God and Jesus. Whenever we pray, we ask for guidance from the Holy Spirit to show us how to lead successful lives and be a better version of ourselves.

Being a part of these women's groups makes me very happy, so I'm very happy about it. I feel fulfilled by our friendships and our spiritual journey together. I appreciate our cultivated positive environment, as we always steer clear of backbiting and negativity and focus on building each other up. Our commitment to loving the Lord and serving Him shapes our discussions and makes our time together meaningful and uplifting. I would not want to go deep into the particular stories about the women in our groups, and I can express my appreciation for the amazing women in our church. I can say with certainty that participating in these groups has become a source of joy and enrichment in my life.

In the past, I distinctly remember that I often turned to my late husband, Andy, for answers, solutions, and comfort; I relied on him rather than seeking guidance from God. While turning to one's spouse is natural, I now recognize that I could have trusted God more for answers. After Andy passed away, I fully turned to God and asked Him to teach me and make me stronger, both mentally and emotionally. Although I still depend on my kids for some things, I have learned to care for myself and make independent decisions. When Andy passed away, I turned completely toward God and relied on Him only, and my faith in Him strengthened even more. I have had a very transformative journey after Andy as I finally learned to make independent decisions, seek God's guidance, and even agree to ask for help when needed.

After Andy, I had to make all the decisions myself, such as where to live, what car to drive, and which bills to pay, so I needed clarity of mind for that. God played a crucial role in helping me easily navigate these challenges. No matter the nature of the decision, I depended solely on God to guide me and give me strength. Even though I had quite an independent spirit, I understood the necessity of accepting help. My daughter has been a tremendous support, but she has her own life with Joe, and I respect that. God has been my constant source of help, especially since I moved closer to my daughter.

While I sometimes wish Andy were still here, I find solace in knowing he is in a much better place and happy in heaven. In my current state, I am confident that I am where I need to be. The church I attend is the right place for me as I am surrounded by some of the best friends I have ever had. God's blessings are pretty evident in my life, and I am grateful for my relationship with God the Father, God the Son (Jesus Christ), and God the Holy Spirit. They continue to care for me and guide me through life's decisions and challenges. While I miss Andy, my faith in God and gratitude for His care remain unwavering.

I can say with absolute certainty that I am extremely grateful to be living a glorious journey and hopefully still in the middle of it. It has been 14 years since Andy passed away, so I would love to have another 14 or 15 years and maybe even stretch it to 20. My mom passed away when she was 97, but I am not sure if I want to live that long; nevertheless, I know that however long I get to live, God is going to be the center of my life. To this day, I love my husband more than anyone I have ever loved in my life. He was always such a pillar of strength for me. I met him when I was 14, and we spent our whole lives together.

It is true that I did have a rotten childhood because the verbal abuse done by my sister had become unbearable for me at one point in time. I had reached my limit of patience and endurance and could not hear anymore. And besides that, the things that my brother did, I didn't even want to think about them again. I clearly remember when my father passed away I was 12 years old; my mother wanted to leave her home and move back to where she grew up. My sister went to college then while my brother joined the army. Mom and I moved back to her native town, where she spent her childhood, and we found a church close to our house.

My life was deeply impacted by that church and the people in it. When I first met Andy, I was only 14 and had not asked Jesus into my heart. On our first date, we went out to eat and then sat by the lake in his car. I was surprised to see him take out the Bible and read a passage to me, and then we prayed together. Andy, who was to be my future husband, was extraordinary. He loved me unconditionally and allowed me to be myself without imposing any sort of expectations. He always gave me the confidence to be vocal in church, which gave me the strength to be myself and trust God to guide my words. Our marriage was filled with love, mutual respect, and a deep affection for our children. It was a unique and wonderful connection I will cherish until my last breath.

My kids have always been amazing when they were little, and I feel so happy seeing that they have grown into terrific adults. I would like to mention that raising them was not an easy task as it came with many challenges, and I am incredibly proud of the individuals that they have grown up to be. Seeing their life accomplishments makes me feel like a successful mother. Both my son and daughter, along with their families, bring immense joy to my life. When my son first got married, it took me a while to adjust to my daughter-in-law and treat her right. But she has been the most incredible daughter-in-law one could ever have and is my constant support. She is now my daughter, and I would like to acknowledge that she is a great mother and a wonderful grandmother.

My son possesses an incredible talent as he is particularly one of the best voices I've heard in church. He speaks as a worship leader there, and his passion reflects something that he probably learned from his father, Andy. I'm grateful for the good life we have had, even though my childhood was really painful. My son's commitment to serving the Lord and the wonderful family he has built fills me with pride and gratitude. Life has had its fair share of ups and downs, but the joy my family brings me makes it all worthwhile.

One very important thing that I can never reiterate enough is the fact that meeting Andy in church marked the beginning of a wonderful new life for me. Falling in love with him, marrying him, and then sharing his life were things I cherish, and I have no regrets about choosing him as my life partner. I love Andy the most in this world; however, my love for God is paramount. With each passing year, I become closer to God, making me more confident. I clearly remember that Andy had great social skills and could talk to anyone, and I always admired him for this reason. Like him, I have also become open to talking to other people. I see it as a positive way to connect with people and do not consider it interference. When I reflect on the past 50 or 60 years of my life, I genuinely appreciate the journey I have been on.

Currently, I find joy in being a good friend to many of the ladies in the church, and I also engage with the men. I am not looking for a romantic relationship, but my main focus is only to be a great friend to people who walk into my life. I value the time I have left in this world and believe it's best spent building meaningful connections and friendships. This journey that has always been guided by God brings fulfillment and purpose to my life.

I have a strong desire to help others by praying for them and offering them any advice or wisdom that God blesses me with. God guided my life's journey, and it has taught me precious lessons. I consider it my duty to share my experiences with other people to make their voyage easy. God was kind enough to bless me with the best husband, children, and even a great-granddaughter. I am extremely happy to be part of my church community, and it is a source of happiness in my life. I cherish the relationships with the wonderful ladies I've come to know. My purpose for the rest of my life is absolutely clear – to serve the Lord, be a witness for Him, and be a prayer warrior and friend to those in the church. My goal is to help others walk closer to God each day. I pray that I'm already making a positive impact in their lives.

The center of my life has now shifted to God, and I want to spend my life in a way that depicts His love and grace. This current phase of my life is a glorious journey, and all the credit goes to God's blessings. My beautiful family, including my husband, daughter, son, grandson, granddaughter, daughter-in-law, and great-granddaughter, fills my heart with love. I am grateful for my church family and the joy I experience daily in this beautiful journey.

My life's expedition has taught me that no matter how tough the circumstances may become, you should never lose hope. There is indeed light at the end of every tunnel. When you decide not to give up and are optimistic about life, you see ways to cope and deal with different situations. Things will start to work out the way you want them to. One thing that everyone should never forget is that God is always there to protect us and pave the way for us when we cannot handle the conditions around us. We must learn to accept finite disappointment but never lose infinite hope and be able to see that there is light and hope despite all of the darkness. I want to end this book on a positive note for my wonderful readers:

Every situation in life is temporary. So, when life is good, make sure you enjoy and receive it fully. When life is not good, remember that it will not last forever, and better days will definitely come.

Made in United States
North Haven, CT
13 May 2024